BUTTERFLIES
DECODING THEIR SIGNS & SYMBOLS

Philip Howse

BUTTERFLIES
DECODING THEIR SIGNS & SYMBOLS

FIREFLY BOOKS

For my wife Susan, for her unfailing support, and to Debbie and Frances

A FIREFLY BOOK

Published by Firefly Books Ltd. 2010

First printing

Publisher Cataloging-in-Publication Data (U.S.)
Howse, Philip.
   Butterflies : decoding their signs & symbols / Philip Howse.
[192] p. : 5 col. ill., 244 col. photos. ; 30 x 24 cm.
Includes index.
Summary: Explores the phenomena of visual perception, illusion and reality,
unveiling the tangled web that insects weave as they employ color and pattern
to deceive and confuse their predators.
ISBN-13: 978-1-55407-773-1
ISBN-10: 1-55407-773-7
1. Insects – Adaptation. I. Title.
595.7 dc22   QL495.H69 2010

Library and Archives Canada Cataloguing in Publication
Howse, P. E. (Philip Edwin)
         Butterflies : decoding their signs & symbols / Philip Howse.
Includes index.
ISBN-13: 978-1-55407-773-1
ISBN-10: 1-55407-773-7
         1. Butterflies--Adaptation. 2. Butterflies--Color. 3. Protective
coloration (Biology). I. Title.
QL562.2.H69 2010   595.78'91472   C2010-901799-4

Published in the United States by
Firefly Books (U.S.) Inc.
P.O. Box 1338, Ellicott Station
Buffalo, New York 14205

Published in Canada by
Firefly Books Ltd.
66 Leek Crescent
Richmond Hill, Ontario L4B 1H1

Published in Great Britain by
Papadakis Publisher
A member of New Architecture Group Ltd.
Kimber Studio, Winterbourne, Berkshire,
RG20 8AN, U.K. www.papadakis.net

Publishing Director: Alexandra Papadakis
Editors: Sheila de Vallée, Sarah Roberts
Designer: Aldo Sampieri

Printed in China

front cover: **Sequential images of the large white butterfly (*Pieris brassicae*) in flight**

back cover: **The Madagascan emperor moth (*Antherina suraka*)**

title page: **Psyche, Wolf von Hoyer, 1842. Neue Pinokothek, Munich.**
"Surely I dreamt today, or did I see The winged Psyche with awaken'd eyes?"
Keats, *Ode to Psyche*

title page: ***Automeris montezuma*, a giant silkmoth from South America**

All images are © Philip Howse with the exception of the images listed below and those in the public domain.

cover image © Kim Taylor/naturepl.com; p2: © Oliver Kurmis; pp3, 142, 168 (top), 181 (right) & back cover: © Kirby Wolfe; pp3, 8, 20, 21, 55, 63 (right), 64, 66-7, 68, 69, 70-71, 72 (top left, top right & bottom), 73, 75, 78 (top & bottom), 80, 81, 82-3, 84 (left & right), 85, 90, 95 (left & right), 96, 97, 99, 100, 102 (left), 104, 120, 122, 123, 126, 128, 135, 136, 137 (left & right), 141, 158, 159 (top), 160 (left & right), 162 (right), 164 (left & right), 166, 167 (top), 173, 178, 180 (all), 182, 184 (right) & 187: © Stratford-upon-Avon Butterfly Farm Ltd; p10: redrawn by the author after Abbé Breuil; p11 (left): © Ugo Bardi; p11 (right): © Marjorie O'Brian; pp12 & 177 (top right): drawn from a photograph in *The Art of Prehistoric Man in Western Europe* by Leroi-Gourhan, Thames & Hudson; pp13, 87 (right), p119 (left), p134: © Jeroen Voogd; p14 (above): Alan Dawson; p14 (right): Alena Chrastová; pp15 (top right), 17 (bottom left), & 79: from Detmold, in *Fabre's Book of Insects*, Hodder & Stoughton, 1925; p17 (top centre) © Lucy Goodison; p18: © John Simmons/Getty Images; p19: © Damian Pinguey; pp22, 23 & 169 (left): © Butterfly World, K. F. Dolbear; pp27, 57, 59, 60, 98 (top), 109 (top left, bottom right & bottom middle) & 153 (left & right): © Mike Bailey & Steve Williams; pp29, 114-115, 117: © Chris Manley; p30: © William Holman Hunt/Getty Images; p33: © Philippe Halsman/Magnum Photos; p34, 54, p75 (bottom) & 163 (right): © Peter Eeles; p35: © Maria Dattola; p36: a plate from *The Aurelian* by Moses Harris, 1776; p38: © Manuel L. Arduengo; p.39: © Alexandra Papadakis; p40: © Zane Edwards; p42: © The National Gallery, London; p43 (top): © AFP/Getty Images; p44: © Andrzej Staskowiak; p45: © Chris Beckett; p48: © Kim Taylor/naturepl.com; p50: © Vince Massimo; p50: © Armando Caldas; p63 (left): © A. Macmillan; p65 (left): © Karen Nichols; p65 (right): author's reconstruction; p74 & 167 (bottom): © Steen Heilesen; pp76-7: © Andy Phillips; p86 (left): © Kevin DuRose; p86 (right): © Jon Ellis, Japan; p87 (left): © Gary Alpert; p87 (bottom right): © Gerry Dudgeon; p92: © Patrick Coin; p93: © Vicki DeLoach; p98 (bottom): © Logo of the University of Southampton Staff Club; p102 (right): © From Venturi: *Michelangelo*, F. Warne, 1928; p103 (left): © Juanjo Rodriguez Camacho; p103 (right): © L. Williamson; p106: © Tom Brereton; p109 (bottom left): © Cor Zonneveld; p112 (left): © Nicholas Ng; p113 (top): © The Tate Gallery & © Succession Marcel Duchamp/ADAGP, Paris and DACS, London 2010; p116 & 184 (left): © Paul Cecil; p118 (top): © M. G. Venkatesha; p118 (middle): used under the Creative Commons license; p118 (bottom): © Amy Shriber 2003; p119 (right): © Alison F. Hunter; p121: © Stavros Markopoulos; p123 (top right): © Tom Murray; p125: © Laurie J Grove; p130: © Iqbal Singh, Saggu, Isha Foundation; p131 (right): © Richard Ishida; p133 (left): © Lynette Schimming; p138: © Solon Morse; p138 (bottom): © P. Morrissey; p141 (bottom): © Ryan M. Moody; p145: © J. Logan; p149 (top): © Kristine Olsen; p149 (bottom): © Andres Egui; p150 (left): © Kian-Peng SIM; p150 (right): © timsmithphotos.com; p152: © The National Gallery, London; p162 (left): © Pete Vukusic, University of Exeter; p163 (left): © Courtesy of Clipper Teas Ltd; p165: © Karen Nichols; p169 (right): © Tony Bamford; p171 (right): © Mike Kempsey; p174 & 176: © Petrina Hughes; p179 (right): © William Quatman; p181 (left): © Frank Wouters; p183: © Raymond Y. Wang, moth by Zdeno Lucbauer; p185: video by Raymond Wang; p186: © Tony Edgecombe; page188 (right): © South Bank Centre, 1992. From *The Art of Ancient Mexico*; p189 (left): © Scott Nelson

We gratefully acknowledge the permission granted to use these images. Every possible attempt has been made to identify and contact copyright holders. Any errors or omissions are inadvertent and will be corrected in subsequent editions.

Contents

" '...those creatures, making honey down there? They can't be bees – nobody ever saw bees a mile off, you know – ' and for some time she stood silent, watching one of them that was bustling about among the flowers, poking its proboscis into them, 'just as if it was a regular bee,' thought Alice. However, this was anything but a regular bee: in fact it was an elephant – as Alice soon found out, though the idea quite took her breath away at first."

Lewis Carroll: *Through the Looking Glass*

Alles Sichtbar ist Ausdruck, alle Natur ist Bild, ist Sprache und farbige Hieroglyphenschrift

(Everything we see is an impression, all nature is pictorial art, is language and colourful heiroglyphic script)

Hermann Hesse: *Ueber Schmetterlinge*, 1935

PREFACE

The work of any artist is in some way a representation of nature, or dreams, or of ideas. Colour, shape, design and sometimes movement create questions in the mind of the observer, which are ultimately resolved, as a young child wrestles with a series of letters which gradually form a word, giving an idea of something, and then an image. A series of symbols has conveyed meaning.

Why, then, do we look at a flower, a bird, or a butterfly, and not see Nature as an artist at work? The burning desire of man to identify, classify, catalogue, and reduce nature to mathematical equations, has closed our eyes to the idea that the beauty we see may also have meaning, if not for us, for many of the animals with which we share the world. The overwhelming appeal of the concept of evolution through natural selection has focussed the minds of generations of biologists on trends, and the similarities and differences between organisms that is grist to the mill of taxonomists. To paraphrase T.S.Eliot, "Where is the imagination that has been lost in knowledge and where is the knowledge that has been lost in information?" This book is an attempt to show that there is a language in the wings of butterflies and moths. A language that we can learn to read, as archaeologists have learnt to interpret the language of symbols from prehistory, as psychologists have learnt to interpret dreams, and as we have all learnt to appreciate art. This does not help us to understand why we see butterflies and moths as creatures that epitomise the beauty of nature, but it underlines what Darwin called the 'grandeur' of evolutionary theory.

This book contains some new ideas about mimicry in insects which may help to explain the evolution of many of the diverse forms and colour patterns of butterflies and moths. Many insects have evolved colourings and shapes which enable them to blend in with features of their feeding and resting places, as in camouflage, or to resemble closely other species of insect that harbour unpalatable toxins (Batesian and Müllerian mimics). Although mimicry of wasps and hornets is fairly common, biologists have generally overlooked the fact that selected features of potentially dangerous vertebrate predators, such as snakes, lizards and mammals, can be identified on the wings of butterflies and moths. I believe that the way in which our visual perception is organised prevents us from seeing these features, and we need to see insects as other animals see them in order to appreciate the significance of their design.

Writing this book has been an exciting process of discovery. As I gradually realised how much our processes of visual perception have been fashioned by experience starting at birth, I tried to create a *tabula rasa* in my mind and see the designs on the wings of butterflies and moths without preconceptions. As a result I have been able to see something new again and again. It is not easy to do this at first, but it gets easier, and I encourage you to persevere. If you do, your initial scepticism may fade and you may see a richness that was hidden to you and which, strangely, only some autistic people normally experience.

You will find that this book is full of speculation which has no experimental support, and many will therefore regard it as unscientific. I make no apology for that: my aim has been to stretch the imagination, as an artist does, to change the reader's perception and understanding of the natural world. I am sustained in this by the fact that even such a monumental work as *The Origin of Species* was published against the advice of the publisher's reviewer that proof was lacking on every page. However, an apology is due to the reader if I leave the impression that there is a golden thread in the following pages that unravels all. There are good sound alternative theories to undermine some of the flimsy edifices I have started to build.

Much fascinating but neglected information about Lepidoptera is found in the writings of the Victorian naturalists, starting with Charles Darwin, Alfred Russell Wallace and Henry Walter Bates. I have also been inspired by the original approach of certain entomologists of the twentieth century such as Fabre, Hinton and the Hon. Miriam Rothschild. The latter stands apart amongst entomologists, and the bases of many of my ideas have come from reading her publications. Significantly, such people were not primarily experimentalists, working in laboratories, but were the keenest of observers.

I am also particularly grateful to the following for their generous help and contributions. First and foremost, Clive Farrell, the creator of 'Butterfly World', for his encouragement and kindness in making available to me the magnificent library of photographs owned by the Stratford Butterfly Farm; Patric Morrissey for filling in some of the enormous gaps in my knowledge of art, and numerous people for generously providing me with exceptional illustrations, especially Lucy Goodison, Chris Manley, Peter Eeles (UK Butterflies), Kirby Wolfe, Steen Heilesen, Jeroen Voogd, Tony Bamford, Petrina Hughes, Mike Bailey, Steve Williams and Gerry Dudgeon. I am indebted to the late Andreas Papadakis for his encouragement and inspiration, to Alexandra Papadakis for her enthusiasm and expertise in design and production, Sarah Roberts for coping with a mountain of images, Sheila de Vallée for editing the manuscript, and, last but not least, to my wife Susan for her support and encouragement.

Finally, I discovered that my personal voyage of discovery in writing this book about Psyche in her various guises was marvellously pictured by Keats' words in his *Ode to Psyche*:

> "Yes, I will be thy priest, and build a fane
> In some untrodden region of my mind,
> Where branched thoughts, new grown with pleasant pain
> Instead of pines shall murmur in the wind."

Echœs *from*
Nature's Temple

"La Nature est un temple où de vivants piliers
Laissent parfois sortir de confuses paroles;
L'homme y passe à travers des forêts de symboles
Qui l'observent avec des regards familiers."

Baudelaire: *Correspondances*

The three sons of Count Bégouën spent much of their time exploring the caves in the foothills of the Pyrenees. Following a stream that led into the Tuc d'Audoubert cave in 1912 they entered a chamber far from the entrance where they found beautiful clay sculptures of bison dating back to 16 000 BC, which are among the greatest treasures from the prehistoric world. Two years later, crawling through a narrow vertical shaft they discovered, in what later came to be known as the *Trois Frères* (three brothers) cave, a remarkable rock painting that was to achieve even greater fame. This was described as a sorcerer by the Abbé Breuil, who was the doyen of scholars of prehistory in the early twentieth century. Both he and Count Bégouën believed that the artist had been practising sympathetic magic to ensure success in hunting.

What is so striking about this figure is that it is a complex human-animal hybrid. Bégouën[i] described it thus:

> "Here we see an amazing masked figure with a long beard, the eyes of an owl, the antlers of a stag, the ears of a wolf, the claws of a lion and the tail of a horse. It is engraved and outlined in black paint, about ten feet from the ground…. It seems to dominate and preside over all the hundreds of creatures, of thirteen different species, engraved and drawn on the walls below. It is the supreme mystery of the cave."

More recently, Ann Baring and Jules Cashford[ii] pointed out that only the feet are definitely human.

> "The whole feeling of the painting confuses the distinction between the human and the animal…. The flowing 'beard' in itself is like a lion's mane, and appears to be a human beard only because of the numinous look in the eyes that it frames, for the most arresting thing about this magnificent god-like being is his expression, which seems to gaze towards you and beyond…"

Some three thousand years later, in the Middle Ages of Europe, stonemasons put gargoyles and

previous page: **The peacock pansy butterfly (*Junonia almana*) on which the ivory figure (page 17) may have been modelled. This butterfly is now found only on the Indian subcontinent, but may have been present further west in Minoan times, contemporaneously with the elephants which probably supplied the ivory**

states of fantastical beasts on the outer walls of churches and cathedrals. These were usually hybrid animals, part bird, snake, lizard, bat, goat, lion, etc. On the wall of the Abbey church of La Sauve Majeure in the Gironde are stone carvings of hybrid mythological beasts: the combat between the aspics and the basilisks. The aspic is a cockerel with the tail of a snake, and a basilisk has the head and legs of a cockerel, the body, tail and tongue of a snake, and bats' wings. Like many figures from the ancient world it symbolised the earth, the air and the ground below. The aspic (the asp that Cleopatra clasped to her bosom) killed with the most venomous bite known to man. It was believed that the basilisk, like the evil eye, could kill just by staring at someone. Pliny the Elder[iii] wrote:

> "Anyone who sees the eyes of a basilisk serpent (basilisci serpentis) dies immediately. ... Its touch and even its breath scorch grass, kill bushes and burst rocks. Its poison is so deadly that once when a man on a horse speared a basilisk, the venom travelled up the spear and killed not only the man, but also the horse."

The only way of killing a basilisk, he recorded, is to throw it down a weasel's hole, where the stinking breath of the weasel proves fatal to it. Ironically, Pliny met his own basilisk in AD 79 when he sailed across the Bay of Naples to investigate the towering cloud of smoke and ash emerging from Vesuvius and hovering over Pompeii and Herculaneum.

Another of the most fearsome creatures of mythology was the *chimaera*. This creature, which is portrayed with all its bizarre and dread-inspiring features in a famous Etruscan sculpture, was described by Hesiod as

> "breathing invincible fire, a great and terrible creature, swift of foot and strong. She had three heads, one of a fierce-eyed lion, the second of a goat, and the third of a snake, a mighty serpent. The lion was in the front, the snake at the rear, and the goat in the middle breathing out a great blast of blazing fire."

opposite: **The Sorcerer of the** ***Trois Frères*** **cave, Arriège, France c. 14 000 BC**

above left: **The chimaera of Arezzo, 4th century BC. Museo Archeologico Nazionale, Florence**

above right: **Basilisk. A sculpture on the Ruthvens Museum Building, University of Michigan. After Aldrovandi, 1642**

above left: **Cave painting of moths from the *Trois Frères* cave, possibly of the eyed hawk moth. The drawing has been made after inverting the photograph as originally printed. 11-14 000 BC**

above right: **Memorial window engraved by Laurence Whistler from St Nicholas church, Moreton, Dorset**

Such fearsome creatures were evil spirit effigies conceived in the imagination of sculptors. They spawned a host of sculptures that adorn ancient cathedrals and churches and inspired gargoyles. The images were used to ward off their like, the devil and evil spirits. Of course they do not exist in nature. Or do they? Perhaps in some form they do, and their bizarre nature serves a purpose.

This book is about insects, although you may be forgiven for wondering if that were so up to this point. If we look back to prehistoric times we find that insects have figured in mythology, and to this day there are some that remain in some senses mythical beasts. In the cave of Le Portel in the Pyrenees, cave paintings about thirteen thousand years old include a design that is highly suggestive of a peacock butterfly with its wings slightly open, although the generally accepted interpretation is that it is a derived female symbol. Perhaps by serendipity, the artist Laurence Whistler portrayed the same insect in a magnificent etched glass window in the church at Moreton in Dorset, where Lawrence of Arabia is buried. This window is a memorial to an airman whose plane was shot down in France during the Second World War, and the butterfly symbolises the ascent of the soul.

So-called brace-shaped or tectiform signs found in the *Trois Frères* cave have also been dismissed as stylised female signs. They are unlikely to represent birds, because *Trois Frères* has an "owl gallery" with clearly recognisable drawings of the birds. But if you change your angle of view by inverting the page of the book[iv] in which the photograph was printed, the drawings become unmistakable insects – hawk moths, perhaps – one showing the division into head, thorax and abdomen, and both having a pair of antennae. The antennae appear particularly long in the larger design, and there are also indications of hind-wings, one of which appears to have an eye-spot on it. The Stone Age artist may have drawn an eyed hawk moth, which has a pair of bright eye-spots on its hind-wings, similar to the eyes of owls (and owls are pictured in the same cave). The significance of the eye as a symbol we will look at later on, but owl goddesses occur in several ancient cultures, so the people of the *Trois Frères* cave may have left these traces of spiritual belief in their art. The eyed hawk is possibly one of the few species with eye-spots recalling owl eyes that was around in southern Europe after the last Ice Age.

The archaeologist Marija Gimbutas revolutionised the interpretation of prehistoric art in her books *The Language of the Goddess* and *Civilisation of the Goddess*,[v] creating a lexicon of over a hundred different symbols from European Stone Age art, many of them connected with fertility and reproduction. These constitute a language in which the meanings of symbols on, say, a piece of

The eyed hawk moth
(*Smerinthus ocellata*) a possible
icon of a Neolithic owl goddess
(see figure opposite, top left)

pottery, interlock, so that one cannot be understood without involving others as in a normal alphabetic language. The earliest known symbols, dating back to Neanderthal man forty thousand years ago, are the inverted chevron (M), which Gimbutas claims represented water (the basis of all life), and the chevron (V), which represented the female pubic triangle. These symbols (if that is indeed what they are) are found everywhere in Neolithic art.

According to Anne Baring and Jules Cashford,[vi] in the early Neolithic and late Palaeolithic eras, many designs dating back twenty-five thousand years to the Neolithic and the late Palaeolithic eras were found featuring the bird goddess, who also represented water and creation. Owl goddess figures became common later – the owl was the bird of the goddess Athene (Minerva), a goddess of the world beyond death. The large eyes signified the goddess's protective role.

We are very aware of the difference between birds and butterflies or moths, but that is because our concepts are based on a knowledge of the anatomy and the systematic grouping of organisms that Linnaeus conceived several hundred years ago. Before that, and for those tribes that today have had no contact with western science, animals have been or are still grouped on simple, or perhaps we should say crude, criteria. Just as non-biologists call any creature from the sea with an external skeleton a 'shell-fish', Aristotle and other early naturalists recognised only 'kinds' of animals, so that little distinction would be seen between those that could fly. In the language of the ancient Chinese, a butterfly was represented by basically the same pictograph as a bird, that is, it was seen as a type of bird (or *vice-versa* perhaps). So we can conclude that an owl and a butterfly or moth with eye-spots could have been regarded as much the same thing, and therefore a butterfly could have been used to represent the bird goddess of the Neolithic cultures.

Butterfly symbols have been found on pots in former Czechoslovakia dating back to the fifth millennium BC. These are some of the symbols of Nature's temple that speak to us, as Baudelaire says to us in his poem *Correspondances*, like "long echoes that form together in a darkening and profound unity." The bee and the butterfly are believed to have symbolised transformation of the soul at death and rebirth: a theme that recurs repeatedly in other civilisations from the Greeks and Romans to the Aztecs, and both death and regeneration are features of a mother goddess, who is in turn a metaphor for nature.

From the Minoan civilisation of 3000 to 1000 BC, images of insects have survived, including bees and butterflies. Both of these acquired mythological and symbolic significance: they were recognised as the agents that fertilised flowers and gave rise to new life in seeds; and the

honeybee had the added kudos of being the producer of honey and the intoxicating liquor made from it. Images of the mother goddess as a queen bee are found engraved on some of the rings and seals that have survived, and are recognisable by the form of the head, which is obviously not human, the limbs, the hourglass body and diminutive wings.

One of the most famous gold ornaments known from antiquity (dated to 2000-1700 BC) was found in a tomb in Minoan Crete and is a pendant in the form of two bees mating beneath a crown, their feet clasping a ball of what may be pollen. The majority view is that they are honeybees[vii] and that the queen bee represented a deity. The cycle of life in the hive, with the bees hibernating during the winter, is generally considered by archaeologists to be a model for death and regeneration. But the gold figures are not necessarily honeybees – they could be other kinds of bee or wasp. People have argued for over fifty years over the identity of the insects: some, including the distinguished entomologist O.W. Richards, were convinced that they are *Polistes* wasps.[viii] These are the paper wasps that are common in the Mediterranean and make very small nests – so the presumed pollen ball may actually be a nest. A more likely explanation, however, is that they are solitary bees, which commonly make a large pollen ball that they put into an underground cell and then lay an egg on it. Their life cycle mirroring death and resurrection is thus analogous to that of the scarab beetles revered by the ancient Egyptians (see below). Coincidentally, a bull-head statue from 4000 BC in Poland described by Baring and Cashford[ix] has a 'bee' traced on it in dots, and this bee reinforces the symbol of resurrection that the bull represents.

It is likely that honeybees were already domesticated in this epoch. Eva Crane, who researched the matter in great detail,[x] traced the use of terracotta hives back to 400 BC in southern Greece, although the Egyptians had apparently domesticated the honeybee by 1450 BC. According to Baring and Cashford, though, bee hives are described in the very early hieroglyphic writing of the Minoans known as 'Linear A' which was used from about 2000 BC. Although there are references to honey in the Bible and there are African cave paintings of people collecting honey, these most probably refer to wild honeybees, and it is likely that the ancient civilisations were more familiar with solitary and subsocial species of bee.

above: **Gold 'bee' pendant from Malia. Old Palace period of Minoan Crete (1800-1650 BC) These may be solitary bees placing eggs on their pollen ball in their underground cell and holding an egg between them, thus providing a metaphor for regeneration similar to that of the scarab beetle. Herakleion Museum, Crete**

right: **The 'Isopata' gold seal ring from ancient Crete , in which the bee goddess (centre) appears to be sowing the seeds of new life. She has a bee-like head with a large eye and antennae, diminutive wings, flattened arms like bee legs, tapering hands and feet like *tarsi* (insect feet), a narrow waist, and a skirt that appears segmented, with a sting at the bottom. The other figures show similar features. One of her 'seeds' is a chrysalis from which a butterfly escapes. Minoan, c.1500 BC. Herakleion Museum, Crete**

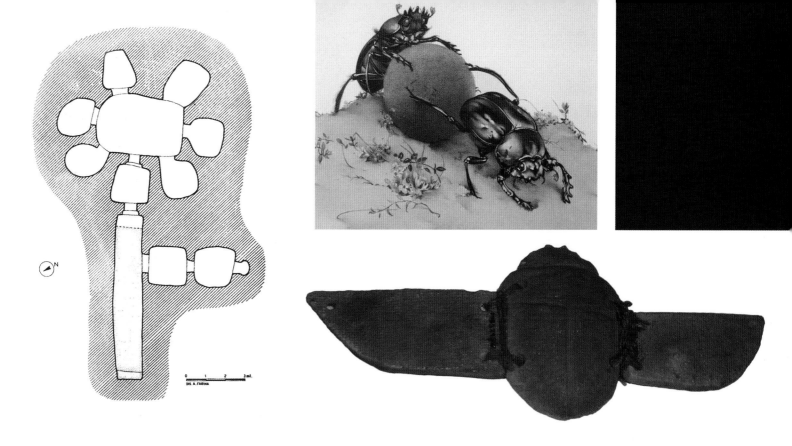

The Minoans also left paintings, pottery and sculptures of bulls' heads on their temples and burial chambers similar to those that have survived in parts of Italy. Sardinia is renowned for its wealth of late Stone Age sites, constructed one to two thousand years before Stonehenge. These underground tombs have a passageway leading to an entrance from which circular burial cells bud out, forming separate dwelling places for the dead that were commonly furnished with provisions for the afterlife. The parallel between this design and that of the nests of some solitary bees is striking. Only the honeybees live in colonies of hundreds to tens of thousands of individuals. There are many other species of bee, including bumble-bees, in which the queen rears only a few offspring, often in underground burrows, that emerge and live for only a few weeks. These are called solitary or subsocial bees, depending on how much the offspring help the queen. Such bees make an underground burrow with cells leading off, which they provision with a paste made from pollen. An egg is laid in each cell and then the entrance is sealed and the female bee dies. The following spring, adult bees emerge from the burrow.

In ancient Egypt, the scarab beetle had a similar symbolic and sacred role. The scarab fashions a ball of dung, which it rolls along to a place where it makes a burrow in the ground. It lays an egg on the dung, which is the food for the developing grub, and with the beginning of the rainy season a new beetle is 'reborn' from below the earth. It becomes evident that insects have, since the beginning of mankind, become part of a lexicon of symbols upon which man's view of spirituality and the meaning of life has been based. Maybe the people of the Sardinian cultures of the 3rd-4th millennia BC were even modelling their necropolises on solitary bees, anticipating the survival of the dead below ground and their resurrection as adult beings in the same way that solitary bees and wasps are 'born' again as new adults after a period underground. The necropolis of Anghelu Ruju consists of underground chambers carved from the solid rock. In the spring and summer you find that you are not alone in the sun, but in the company of hunting wasps and solitary bees. Their activities – provisioning their subterranean nest chambers, sealing them up and then disappearing to reappear in the same form again in the future – cannot help but magnify the suggestion that that the necropolises were constructed with the intent of conjuring the same kind of result. The entrances to their underground tombs are marked with bulls' heads carved into the rock and painted on the walls. The bull was revered throughout the Aegean from at least Neolithic times as a source of energy and new life. Virgil, among others, perpetuated the belief that bees were created from the bodies of bulls that had been sacrificed. Some Minoan artefacts show lilies growing from the bodies of bulls and butterflies arising between the horns. Hence there was a conflation of several iconic and symbolic images; the bull, the bee, the flower, the butterfly, and the sacrificial axe, which often took the

clockwise from top left: **Plan of Neolithic necropolis resembling the nest of primitive social bees. Anghelu Ruju, Sardinia**

Scarab beetles burying their ball of dung, the food store for their larvae. New adults will appear next season, 'resurrected' from these subterranean tombs

A winged scarab from the Egyptian 8th Dynasty (1567-1320 BC) found in a Neolithic hoard at Bath. The wings symbolise a safe journey to the afterlife and the blue colour signifies regeneration. Pump Room Museum, Bath

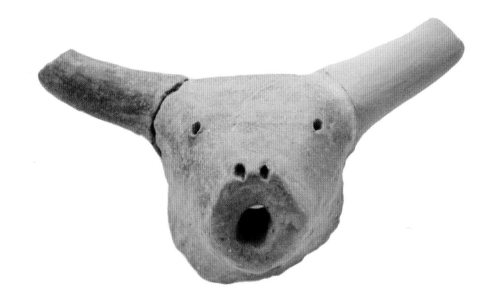

place of the butterfly image that it resembled. Marija Gimbutas[xi] shocked the world and upset the archaeological establishment with her theory that the bulls' heads were sexual symbols, not emblems of male power and strength as had been taken for granted by most people, but representations of the female reproductive organs. The head of the bull, especially the type figured by the Minoans, she realised, had a remarkable similarity to the shape of a uterus with the horns representing the fallopian tubes. The heads are thus understood in this context to have been symbols of fertility and rebirth rather than expressions of masculinity or a male god, which they appear to be in other aspects of the same culture.

A pottery vessel from the same era is engraved with a design showing a ritual or dance scene in which the dancers are represented as butterflies. The triangular symbolic forms of the dresses are complemented with the outstretched arms which figure the butterfly antennae. These are remarkably similar to painted images found in a shrine from the ancient Anatolian city of Çatal Hüyük which date back about 4000 years earlier, and to the double-axe images that were common in Minoan Crete. They are, again, remarkably similar to images painted on a wall at Velez Blanco (Almeria) dating to 4000 BC, which have been interpreted as a flight of red butterflies, or birds.[xii]

One of the oldest designs of a butterfly from the early Minoan era (1600 BC) rises above the horns of a bull and has two eye-spots and a human head with a crown, and birds' feet. The butterfly, the owl and the bull were thus fused together in an image invoking the concepts of rebirth from the sacred womb, the soul, death and the afterlife. For the Minoans the butterfly (or

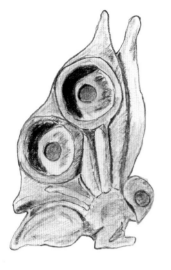

moth) represents the soul – a theme adopted by the Aztecs four thousand miles away and over two thousand years later, and which was carried forward into Greek and Roman culture to survive until relatively recent times.

Early in the last century a peasant stumbled upon an engraved gold disk in a bee hive tomb in south-western Greece, near Pylos. Eventually, the archaeologist Sir Arthur Evans, famous for his excavation of Knossos, heard about this find and tracked the treasure down to this remote part of Greece. It became known as the 'Ring of Nestor'. Although the authenticity of this ring has recently been challenged, Evans was overwhelmed by its detail and beauty. He wrote that this 'ring' gave the first glimpse of the world beyond, as conceived by the Minoans. The scene includes a wealth of symbols, central to which are the Tree of Life and the Mother Goddess, and can be interpreted as a description of religious and spiritual life based on 'interlocking symbols'. Part of the scene represents the afterlife, and shows two seated figures with chrysalises and two butterflies hovering above them. Evans interpreted them as an allusion to the resurgence of the human spirit after death, and wrote:

> *"We see here, reunited by the life-giving power of the Goddess and symbolised by the chrysalises and butterflies, a young couple whom death had parted."*[xiii]

One of the couple was supposedly the owner of the disk and had lost his wife – evidently he had been a wealthy merchant who could afford such a commemorative work of art, while possibly not imagining that its fame would last five thousand years or more!

The butterfly image underwent its own metamorphosis in that epoch to become a double-bladed axe, known as a *labrys*. Labrys axes adorned what were believed to be dancing floors in temples, and gave their name to *labyrinths*. No one knows for certain why a labyrinth came to be another word for a kind of maze, although it has been suggested that the maze is a diagram of the choreography of the dance. The labrys is a common symbol in Minoan art and may have been used as a sacrificial knife, but not as a weapon, for the Minoans were considered to be

above, right hand side: **A Minoan wooden sarcophagus, decorated with labrys axes between lily leaves. These are obvious symbols of regeneration in which the double axes appear to represent butterflies and flowers at the same time. c. 1300-1100 BC. Rethymnon Archaeological Museum, Crete**

Another Minoan image on a sarcophagus from the necropolis at Armeno in Crete in which the butterfly is replaced with the symbolic double axe. Late Minoan period, 1400–1200 BC. Rethymnon Archaeological Museum, Crete

a very peaceful people. The double-bladed axe was thus a symbol of death, as a blade, and of the soul, as a butterfly. It is possible, then, to make a connection between the butterfly dancers of Sardinia and the butterfly symbols of the Minoans. A similar double-triangle symbol found on pottery from the former Czechoslovakia is the oldest known butterfly symbol, dating back to around 6000 BC.

The ancient Greeks and Romans adopted many of the Minoan beliefs about butterflies after the Minoan civilisation died out following a calamitous volcanic eruption. This led to the legend of Psyche. Psyche was a stunningly beautiful maiden, the mortal lover of Cupid (Eros), who visited her only in the night hours. In the legend, which is found in *The Golden Ass* by Apuleius, Psyche is deceived by her envious sisters into breaking her vow to Cupid not to look on him in the light. When she does this, Cupid disappears, and Psyche's search for him involves avoiding numerous traps set for her by the gods. Psyche's adventures mirror the soul's journey through life. She is said to represent beauty, which unites with desire, leading to pleasure in the form of a mystical union after death and the birth of a daughter whose name is *Voluptas* (pleasure). Psyche has been represented many times in ancient as well as baroque and romantic art as a beautiful girl with butterfly wings. The word *psyche* was used by Aristotle and comes from the ancient Greek word for breath or the soul, *psukhe*, which is also connected through roots in old German and Gothic with the word *aiolos* meaning coloured or iridescent.[xiv] These words can also signify 'butterflies', so 'psychology' could equally well denote the study of butterflies, rather than the cumbersome term 'lepidopterology' that is sometimes used! The symbolic image of Psyche often overlaps with that of Titania (Queen of the Fairies) and Circe in Homer's *Odyssey*, who seduced Odysseus and transformed his followers into animals with a magic potion made from herbs. The artist John Simmons' portrait of Titania (from A *Midsummer Night's Dream*) shows her with the wings of the emperor moth, searching for herbs.

Whilst butterflies seem to have had an important spiritual significance during the Stone Age and subsequent millennia connected with regeneration and rebirth of the spirit, moths, in contrast, were seen as markers of death, or impending death. They generally have sombre colours, fly at night, and were connected with the death goddess. Marija Gimbutas tells us that the Death Goddess of the Stone Age survives as a witch-like old hag in European cultures (e.g. in myths and fairy tales). The word 'nightmare' comes from an old Germanic word, *mora* or *mara*, meaning 'terror', or 'moth'. It is perhaps not a coincidence that many of the larger moths have large eye-spots on their wings, resembling the eyes of owls, the owl being a goddess connected with death. There is a parallel in the New World, where owls figure in the creation myth of the ancient Maya and are deities attendant on the supreme creator.

The butterfly, or moth – usually the common silkworm – was re-adopted by the Christian Church as a symbol of death and rebirth of the soul. Indeed, Maraleen Manos-Jones in her book

opposite: **A painting by John Simmons depicting Titania, Queen of the Fairies, with the wings of an emperor moth**

above: **A female emperor moth, (*Saturnia pavonia*), the origin of the wings of Titania in the preceding figure**

above: **Metamorphosis. The Indian moon moth (*Actias selene*), a giant silk moth, expanding its wings on emergence from the chrysalis tomb from which, using St. Teresa's metaphor, it was 'reborn' after a 'humble life' as a caterpillar**

opposite: **The imago or 'perfect insect': the moon moth ready for flight**

The Spirit of Butterflies[XV] records that in the fifth century AD Pope Gelasius issued a decree defining Christ as a caterpillar. He was seen by that Pontiff as having lived a humble worm-like life and having been resurrected miraculously from the tomb of the chrysalis.

The great sixteenth century religious mystic St. Teresa of Ávila wrote a book called *The Interior Castle* in which she described her inward spiritual journey as a process of metamorphosis. She found the metamorphosis of the silkworm miraculous. She believed that the caterpillar, after a life of constant toil, died in the cocoon and was reborn as the beautiful moth, making a metaphor of how the human soul could be reborn again in Christ.

In Europe and the Old World the moth most closely associated with death is the eponymous death's head hawk moth, primarily because of the white skull-like emblem embroidered on its thorax. This is the insect that stimulated the research that has led to this book. I first found one in the Camargue, photographed it, and then puzzled over the photograph for many years until, after various encounters with surrealistic art, I realised that I had to re-atune my processes of visual perception in order to understand the meaning of markings on butterflies and moths.

The death's head hawk moth does not occur in the New World, but another moth there has become associated with death and rebirth. This is the giant silk moth *Rothschildia*, which the Aztecs called the 'obsidian knife butterfly' (*la mariposa de navajas* in Spanish). This is not, of course, a butterfly, but the issue of whether an insect is a butterfly or a moth is neatly solved in most Latin languages, because the same word usually covers both. In Spanish it

is *mariposa*, which derives from *Maria* (i.e. the Virgin Mary) and *pousar*, meaning to alight – Holy Mary comes to earth – an allusion that some writers have compared with the interpretation of evidence from the Neolithic period for a belief that the Mother Goddess regenerated life on earth. This giant moth has a transparent triangular 'window' in each wing, which the Aztecs saw as a representation of the broad obsidian knife blades used to make human sacrifices. The knife 'butterfly' was transmogrified into a Goddess associated with death, but a swallowtail butterfly, *Papilio semicaudata*, symbolised more definitively the survival of the soul and regeneration of life.

While it is not difficult to appreciate how butterflies and bees have become icons or metaphors for the soul and its survival, and regeneration of the body, the main reasons for the evolution of designs and symbols on the bodies of butterflies and moths have never been seriously considered.

Is there a language of interlocking symbols, like those of the European Neolithic peoples, in which the context of each figure influences the meaning? And then the biggest question of all: why do we, as humans, see symbols like the eyes on an insect's wings, the skull on a death's head hawk moth, or the knife blade on a silk moth's wing, when those features cannot be seen in any way to help the survival of the species? We are forced to the view, reluctantly perhaps, that those symbols were not designed for us. But then, why do they have meaning for us? This leads us to a mystery that Darwin had to confront. He initially tried to explain the colours on butterflies' wings as sexual signals, fashioned by natural selection to ensure that females mated only with males of their own species. This also explained why often it is only the male that bears bright colours, and not the female, because she is the one who makes the choice of partner. But he realised that this was, at best, only a partial answer.

Sexual differences in the Adonis Blue butterfly (*Polyommatus bellargus*). Darwin's explanation for the vivid colours of the male is that the females tend to choose the more brightly coloured males. The males then sacrifice their concealing colour patterns for greater powers of sexual attraction

Dragons
in their Pleasant
Palaces

"By some called Caput Mortuum, or Dead-Head, from the mark on the back, which much resembles a dead Scul.... but the Aurelian society chuse to distinguish it by the name of Bee-Tiger, but for what reason I know not"

Moses Harris: *The Aurelian*, 1766

"Here the beastly harpies make their nests, who chased the Trojans from the Strophades, making dire predictions of what is to come. Wide wings they have, and necks and faces human, legs with claws, and a fat feathered belly, making woeful cries in their strange trees"

Dante: *The Inferno*, Canto XIII

The sinister and bizarre death's head hawk moth is a huge insect that is a living embodiment of a basilisk, aspic, harpy, satyr, sphinx, centaur, griffin, dragon or chimaera. Like those mythical beasts it presents itself as a compendium of several different creatures. What makes it a supreme enigma is the image of skull and cross bones marked in white on its thorax. Some also recognise the backbone and ribs of a skeleton marked in black on the yellow abdomen. It is a creature that, to us, carries inferences of death, darkness and the underworld, and can lead people to panic on seeing it. Why is that? Why has it acquired such fearful symbolism in the course of evolution? There are few more potent symbols than that of a skull, but why is that image, with accompanying cross bones, displayed on a sinister-looking moth? This is a creature that also has its abdomen banded in bright yellow, like some monster wasp, and that makes a piping or squeaking noise, which among the superstitious in earlier times was regarded as speech that no one could understand. Evolution favours features that aid survival and the production of more offspring, but the death's head no more needs to protect itself from man than any other moth, and what meaning can the skull emblem have for its real enemies – birds, lizards, and small mammals?

This book is not so much about the natural history of butterflies and moths, it is about illusion and reality; it is about the ways in which we perceive visual images, compared with the ways in which animals see things, and about the roots of surrealist art in nature and the tangled web that animals weave, employing colour and pattern to deceive. The spark that ignited this interest in insects is etched in my childhood memories; my mother calling me in from the garden to see a red admiral she had caught in a jam-jar. The 'red admiral' turned out to be a small tortoiseshell, but the awe that came upon me on seeing in a few frozen moments the beauty of an insect's wings at close quarters awoke an interest that from then on eclipsed all others.

This seminal encounter led to the discovery of a myriad of never-ending wonders: orange-tips in the hedgerows, browns in the meadows, clouded yellows in the autumn fields, red admirals in the pear tree, hawk moths in the poplar, bright tiger moths in wayside ditches and underwing moths with coloured cloaks on bark. Breeding giant silk moths that came from exotic places revealed the miracle of metamorphosis, and observing their behaviour at the (then) innocent age of eight led me to deduce, among other wonders, the principles of sexual intercourse. The never-ending trail leading to encounters with new insect species, curious forms and colour patterns, to new understandings of behaviour and evolution, and ultimately, to ways of controlling pests by exploiting behaviour, took me into European mountains and vineyards, Indian coffee

plantations and silk farms, Mexican orchards, African savannas and Amazonian forests. But whatever the problem that needed to be solved – reducing the ravages of fruit flies in citrus orchards, of coffee stem borers, or the depredations of leaf-cutting ants, termites or locusts – the butterflies and moths continued to fascinate me above all because of the beauty of their colours and design. The wings of butterflies and moths seemed to form a canvas upon which nature painted indecipherable images of precious and infinite novelty, overwhelming in their variety and perfection. But the questions that arose in my mind time and time again were, 'Why are there so many vivid colour patterns?' 'What do they mean?' 'What purpose do they serve in nature?' Henry Bates,[i] a contemporary of Darwin who gave his name to a form of mimicry in animals, suggested that the wings of butterflies formed a tablet on which nature writes the story of the modification of the species. Alfred Russell Wallace, who developed the theory of evolution by natural selection contemporaneously with Darwin, added to this, and stated his bewilderment thus:

> "..she [Nature] has used them like the pages of some old illuminated missal, to exhibit all her powers in the production, on a miniature scale, of the utmost possibilities of colour-decoration, colour-variety, and of colour-beauty; and has done this by a method which appears to be unnecessarily complex and supremely difficult, in order perhaps to lead us to recognise some guiding power, some supreme mind, directing and organising the blind forces of nature in the production of life and loveliness."[ii]

It is convenient for taxonomists and collectors that butterflies and moths can be grouped into families (swallowtails, browns, yellows, blues, hawk moths, silk moths, etc.), each species sharing some features of a pictorial code. But how do you interpret those hieroglyphs? Do they represent objects or symbols as in ancient Egyptian scripts, which are read by other creatures and about which we still know nothing?

Carl Jung has taught us more about symbols and their meaning in human life than anyone else. He believed that the human psyche has a shadow side that we need to recognise for our own health and survival; it influences our conscious motives through an unconscious in which lurk archetypal images that tend to populate our dreams. He believed that the human mind was constrained by the effects of events in our far distant past so that we have a special sensitivity to certain types of image, which then have a subliminal influence on our behaviour. Sometimes we may fabricate them in our dreams. He explained his concept of the archetype using the analogy

The small tortoiseshell butterfly (*Aglais urticae*), common in suburban gardens and hedgerows in Britain throughout the summer. The meaning of the intricate colour patterning at first sight appears as enigmatic as that of the death's head hawk moth

of a crystal forming in a liquid. The material is the same but discrete structures form within it over time. They form a framework for images that have had meaning for us and have dominated our lives from prehistoric eras. We become aware of the archetypes as symbols – which represent something more than the objects they are, whether they are fruit, animals, geometrical designs, genital organs, objects like the apple, the snake, the cross, the lion, the butterfly, the circle, the eye, the phallus, and so on, and these symbols assist the unconscious to find expression in art, and they mould our perception of the exterior world and our responses to others.

What little we know is only a series of signposts to deeper mysteries, about how we see things and how we interpret what the eye and other senses tell us, but we cannot and must not assume that we see images and interpret those images in the same way as animals do. That is anthropocentricity, which is full of pitfalls, making it is easy to believe that animals, especially furry ones, have the consciousness, and the unconscious, that we have, together with the concepts of good and evil, and that they have beliefs that are linked to symbolic images. True, research has shown that the higher primates such as chimpanzees and gorillas have learning abilities and affective behaviour similar to four-year-old children, but the comparative study of animal behaviour (ethology), which began in earnest with the work of Lorenz and Tinbergen after the last world war, has shown us that animals lower in the evolutionary scale (birds, insects, reptiles, etc.) do not interpret visual images and other sensory stimuli in the same way that we do. They respond as if they see only certain details that are 'meaningful' to them, and not the whole of the image that falls on the retina. The enigmatic death's head hawk moth provides us with an opportunity to look at symbols, meaning, and chimaeric images in the animal world and in our own world. Surprising differences emerge.

The death's head hawk moth was probably known to the ancient Greeks and the Romans from its habit of invading bee hives and stealing the honey. According to Robert Graves,[iii] the inhabitants of Minoan Crete were bee-keepers, using hives made of terracotta. They were plagued by the *Ceraphis*, which literally means 'bee-moth' but which Graves understood to be a kind of locust. There are several species of wax moth that feed on the wax of honeybee combs that are often called bee-moths, but they are only about the size of a clothes moth. Only the death's head is of a size to be compared with a locust.

It is perhaps not surprising that the great Linnaeus named the creature that we know as the death's head hawk moth, the French as the *Tête-de-mort*, the Germans as the *Totenkopfschwärmer*, and the Spanish as *Esfinge de la muerte* or *calavera*, as *Acherontia atropos*, a name with its origins in ancient Greek mythology connecting with the soul and the underworld.

Acheron means 'river of woe'. For the Greeks this was one of five rivers flowing to the underworld, tributaries of the poison-laden river Styx across which the blind ferryman Charon ferried souls after death. People's lives were controlled on a thread by the three fates, Clotho, Lachesis and Atropos. The thread of life is spun on Clotho's spindle, measured by Lachesis's rod, and finally cut by the shears of the most terrible and feared of the fates, Atropos, terminating life. So Linnaeus epitomised the sinister reputation of the moth in its scientific name, *Acherontia atropos*, and he also used 'Lachesis' and 'Styx' in the scientific names of the separate species of death's head hawk moth that occur in the Orient.

The journey of dead souls in Greek mythology, like the adventures in Lewis Carroll's *Alice's Adventures in Wonderland*, involved passage to the underworld, entry, and encounters with fantastical creatures. While Alice needed a golden key to enter the world she then encountered, the ghosts of the Greek dead were endowed by relatives with a coin placed under the tongue to pay the ferryman. When they reached the far bank, which was guarded by the three-headed dog Cerberus, they were eventually directed down one of three paths. The unfortunate ones finished up in the punishment fields ruled over by the god Hades. There, the Erinnyes or Furies punish the guilty for crimes of insult, violence or disobedience to parents. The Erinnyes were the companions of Hecate, goddess of witches, who had three heads and bodies: lion, dog and mare; they were old crones with snakes for hair, dogs' heads, coal-black bodies, bats' wings, and blood-shot eyes. Robert Graves describes them as "personified pangs of conscience". The Erinnyes may be seen as fearful symbolic masquerades representing the pain of guilt in the unconscious.

Death's head hawk moth with hind-wings partially displayed presenting the yellow and black colours associated with wasps

overleaf: *The Hireling Shepherd*, a painting rich in symbolism by Victorian artist William Holman-Hunt. The shepherd, while distracting the shepherdess from her duties, holds a death's head hawk moth in his outstretched left hand

When the death's head is at rest on, for example, a tree trunk, the dark coloured forewings are folded over the rest of its body, so the insect is well camouflaged, blending into the bark. When you attempt to touch it or pick it up, it splays open its black legs and walks slowly like a huge black spider. It may then career about, flapping its wings and leaning from side to side exposing its bright yellow hind-wings and tiger-striped body. At the same time it makes a shrill piping noise, and occasionally a lower pitched sound. It has all the attributes of an evil spirit: a dark-shrouded creature that flies in the night, can suddenly appear, it seems, out of nowhere, change its form, make noises, and display a skull and crossbones.

In previous ages the death's head hawk moth was liable to cause panic. It is recorded that in some areas of Europe it was seen as a messenger of death because its appearance often coincided with the development of an epidemic disease. The French entomologist Louis Figuier[iv] wrote that in country places in England

> "this ominous inhabitant of the air is in league with witches. … It goes and murmurs into [people's ears] with its sad and plaintive voice the name of the person whom death is soon to carry off."

The French themselves in the Middle Ages believed that the dust from the wings of the moth would cause blindness if it got into your eyes.

In England, the moth had the name 'whispering ghost' in some regions. The Victorian chronicler of natural history, the Rev. J.G. Wood, was very amused by a whole circle of panic-stricken village people who had gathered around a death's head hawk moth that had found its way into a churchyard.

> "Not one of them dared touch it, and at last it was killed by the village blacksmith, who courageously took a long jump and came down on the unfortunate Moth with his iron-shod boots."[v]

But in some cultures the insect has been regarded as an ally, protecting against evil, perhaps in the same way that mythical beasts and fearsome gargoyles were believed to protect churches and cathedrals in the Middle Ages. According to Manos-Jones, who records in her book *The Spirit of Butterflies* the earliest occurrence of a portrayal of the moth on the sarcophagus of one of the Egyptian pharaohs, the moth was believed to have magical properties, capable of banishing evil spirits, ghosts, fearsome apparitions and vampires.

In 1850 the Victorian artist William Holman Hunt painted a scene entitled *The Hireling Shepherd*. He was inspired by a line from Shakespeare's *King Lear*, and the aim of his painting was to criticise the clergy of the country for neglecting their pastoral duties. The shepherd is portrayed with his right arm around a young shepherdess who is feeding a lamb with unripe apples (which are not good for them). In the palm of his outstretched right hand he is holding something that on close inspection turns out to be a death's head hawk moth. Salvador Dalí saw this picture, and was inspired to use the moth as a symbol in his art.

Dalí was fascinated by the ability of someone who suffers from paranoia to develop delusions of their visual world and tried to develop or recreate their visions. He wrote:

> "By way of a clear paranoiac process, it becomes possible to receive a double image of perception: that is, the depiction of an object, that without the least physical or anatomical change is simultaneously the depiction of another wholly different object."[vi]

Dalí put another slant on this when he said, "There is only one difference between a madman and me. I am not mad." But he did admit that he was the first to be surprised and often terrified by the images he produced. His principal aim in life was to shock, and he did this in every way he could conceive of: not just on canvas, but in his own appearance, his scandalous behaviour and eccentricities.

Dalí made a surrealist film in 1928 with the famous film director, Luis Buñuel, called *Un Chien Andalou* (An Andalusian Dog). This film, according to Buñuel, was made with the rule that it would involve no idea or image that was capable of rational explanation, and would include only what was irrational or surprising. It starts with a woman's head being grasped from behind

and her eyes are then slit with a razor. Later, a murder takes place in a room, the scene shifts to a park, and then the events unfold as in the following extract from the film script:[vii]

Dalí in Voluptate Mors.
A photograph by Philippe Halsman of Salvador Dalí with a skull composed of naked women

> "And we return to the same room. A door, the one where the hand was caught, opens slowly. The girl we know appears. She closes the door behind her and watches attentively the wall against which the murderer stood. The man is no longer there. The wall is intact, without any furniture or decoration. The girl makes a gesture of vexation and impatience. The wall reappears; in the middle of it there is a small black spot. This small spot, seen up close, is a death's head moth. Full closeup of the moth. The death's head on the moth's wings covers the whole screen."

Salvador Dalí produced a gouache painting entitled *Female bodies as a skull* in which he grouped the naked bodies of women to form the image of a skull when viewed from a sufficient distance. The photographer Philippe Halsman then used this in his portrait of Dalí, called *Dalí in Voluptate Mors* (Dalí in Voluptuous Death). This image of a skull was then used by the makers of the film *The Silence of the Lambs* and superimposed on the 'skull' of a death's head hawk moth, which was subsequently used on posters for the film and for the dust-jacket of Thomas Harris's book. Few people will have noticed this. If you have a copy of a post-film edition of the book, take a look at the skull marking with a lens and you will see a group of naked women. The central image, between the two eye sockets of the skull has been interpreted as a reference to the crucifixion. The moth, which in the poster of *The Silence of the Lambs* covers the woman's lips, appears to be rendering her incapable of expressing her thoughts. In the film, the psychopathic murderer has a habit of leaving the chrysalis of a death's head in the mouth of his victims as a kind of calling card, as symbolic as it is gruesome.

In a famous scene in the film, hundreds of moths are released into a room with Hannibal Lecter. The making of this film in the USA was, however, hampered by the fact that the moth does not occur in North America, so an alternative species of the right size had to be substituted. Fortunately, many American research laboratories rear cultures of a closely related hawk moth called the tobacco hornworm, which is used for research into insect physiology, and can be easily reared on tobacco and rubber plants. The lack of the skull and crossbones markings was not important as the moths were filmed in flight. The insect used in the posters and other publicity

The red admiral (*Vanessa atalanta*), sometimes associated with death in the Middle Ages because of the red (blood) and black (darkness and night) colours

was a 'set' death's head with its wings fully displayed in the conventional (but unnatural) way used for all scientific collections, and adorned with the *Voluptate Mors* emblem.

Another symbolic use of the death's head moth is in Susan Hill's highly acclaimed book, *I'm the King of the Castle*.[viii] A young boy explores a room in his grandfather's house. His grandfather, who was an entomologist with an international reputation, has recently died, leaving a room full of his valuable collection of butterflies and moths. The boy opens a cabinet, and as stale-smelling air comes out of the case his eyes are drawn to the largest moth in the centre of the case:

> "*Acheroptia* [sic] *atropos — though he could only just make out the writing on the card, the ink had faded to a dark yellow in the sun. 'Death's Head Hawk Moth'. He stretched out his hand, put his finger under the head of the pin and slid it up, out of the thick, striped body. At once the whole moth, many years dead, disintegrated, falling into a soft formless heap of dark dust.*"

Moths become a threatening symbol of death, and, along with other forms of psychological torture, the boy uses them to intimidate his sensitive and impressionable friend with ultimately disastrous consequences.

Enigmatically, some references in literature to 'death's head moths' are to insects that are completely different. Thus the red admiral butterfly was associated with death in the Middle Ages, possibly because of its black wings, highlighted with red bands, the colour of blood. Vincent van Gogh's painting of a death's head moth in fact depicts the great peacock moth, which he found in the garden of the asylum he was in. In a letter he describes how he was captivated by its colours, but had to kill it to draw it. He shows it with a black thorax and rib and backbone pattern on the abdomen, which suggests that combining these features with the staring eye-spots on the wings, he was reminded of a skull. Three years earlier, he had painted the *Skull of a skeleton with burning cigarette*, a grey and despairing image.

This use of the death's head in art and literature highlights the psychological impact of the skull image which makes it symbolic of the shadow side of human existence, connecting with occult beliefs, death, hell, and spiritual supremacy. This very powerful symbol is carried by a sinister-

looking moth that flies with the other creatures of the night and provokes a high level of superstition. But the intrigue of the moth does not stop there; it has a mysterious association with honeybees. It is able to enter their hives and steal the honey without being harmed itself, which gave rise to its earlier name of the 'bee tiger', used in one of the first accounts of the moth, which appeared in a famous entomological work prized for its beautiful illustrations, *The Aurelian*, by Moses Harris, published in 1766. The moth was called a tiger (Tyger) because of the yellow and black bands on its abdomen.

The ability to enter and leave beehives unscathed was thought to be more remarkable than the skull pattern, and it was known that the moth produced piping noises that were thought to calm the bees in the same way as the piping of the queen bee. Only relatively recently has it been possible to explain why the moths are not stung and torn apart by honeybees in the same way as other intruders, and that depends not on visual mimicry but on chemical mimicry. Insects are incredibly sensitive to chemicals, sometimes detecting them down to the level of a few molecules. Every species of insect carries its identity, analogous to a thumbprint or DNA scan, in the form of a blend of chemical markers in the waxy layer on the surface of its body. Bees (and other social insects including wasps, ants, and termites) cannot only tell whether another insect they come into contact with is another bee or not, but whether it is a bee from their own or from another hive. The death's head has evolved an amazing chemical camouflage: its chemical signature is virtually identical to that of the average honeybee. It is such a successful robber, that in the Cape Verde Islands where it is abundant it constitutes a serious threat to apiculture.

The hawk moth is also feared because of its size and blackish wings and because it flies at night; thus it can easily be mistaken for a bat. Many superstitions attach to creatures that fly at night; in Celtic folklore to see anything flying at night was considered an evil omen. The devils, witches and evil spirits of the underworld have been associated with night in most cultures. In medieval Christian art the devil is often shown with bat wings. The Mayans of Central America had a bat god, Camazotz, who guarded the entrance to the underworld. The vampire bats of South America, which have given rise to the Dracula legend, are feared for their habit of sucking blood, but they are a serious threat to life in another way, which is their ability to transmit rabies.

The great peacock moth (*Saturnia pyri*) which Van Gogh painted, believing it to be a death's head hawk moth

Mr Harris ad Vivum Sculp.^t

To my Ingenous Friend and Benefactor Mr Dru Drury
This Plate is most Humbly Dedicated by his Obliged Servant Moses Harris

Curiously, bats are seen quite differently in other cultures, particularly in the Far East. The Chinese philosopher Wu Lu used an emblem of five bats around a fruit tree, symbolising the five desirable conditions of human life: health, wealth, happiness, longevity, and a peaceful death. As with the death's head it appears that a fearsome symbol can either signify evil and misfortune, or, like mythical beasts and tribal masks, be used to ward off evil influences.

The moth is a creature that belongs to the category of mythical beasts. It is not mythical, but may appear to us as part bat, part giant wasp, part squeaking mouse, part moth, and (most significantly) part devil: a messenger from hell. It has an affinity with the Harpies of Hades depicted by Dante, who, like the Erinnyes, tormented souls of the living and the dead. It is a miniature dragon.

It is worth recalling at this point that the dragon is a very powerful symbolic concept that has become a fundamental part of Chinese culture. The Chinese dragon is said to be a hybrid of nine animals: the horns of a deer, a camel's head, the devil's eyes, a snake's neck, the abdomen of a large cockle shell, the scales of a carp, the claws of an eagle, the paws of a tiger, and the ears of an ox. It seems that the dragon is capable of almost everything. It can fly, live in the ocean, make rain and control floods. As a result of its omnipotence, it became a kind of deity and the symbol of the Chinese nation.

For some strange reason, perhaps because of association with the stag which has mythical significance, the stag beetle took the role of the scarab in medieval Europe. In Albrecht Dürer's famous painting, this insect, which in Germanic folklore was believed to be capable of overcoming the dragon, was symbolically equated with Christ. According to the Getty Museum, "Seen up close, the creature's legs and spiky mandibles suggest its kinship to imaginary beasts in late Gothic depictions of Hell or the temptation of Saint Anthony Abbott."

These comparisons between mythical animals and insects raise a host of questions about the ways in which the death's head hawk moth, and others like it, affect our perception and that of the animals that share its environment, and about the meaning of all the apparent symbols that we detect, or think we detect, on the wings of butterflies and moths.

opposite: **The Bee Tiger, as the death's head hawk moth was once known. A plate from** *The Aurelian* **by Moses Harris (1776)**

below: **Chinese dragon, with features of many different animals, outside the Burmese Buddhist temple in Penang, Malaysia**

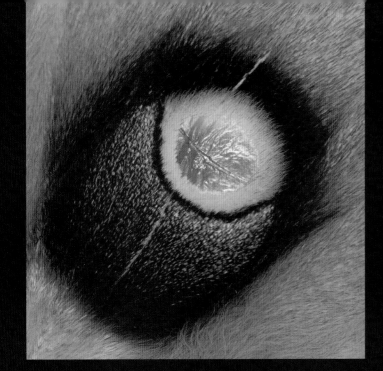

Skulls & Symbols

"All art is at once surface and symbol.
Those who go beneath the surface do so at their peril.
Those who read the symbol do so at their peril.
It is the spectator, and not life, that art really mirrors."

Oscar Wilde: *The Picture of Dorian Gray*

"Alas, poor Yorick. I knew him, Horatio."

Shakespeare: *Hamlet*

We have a special ability to recognise faces, which we can assume has been of great importance in the evolution of human social behaviour. Perhaps because of this, the skull, which is a template, like a partially developed photographic print of a marble head, has a magnetic attraction for us.

Hamlet, contemplating the skull of his long-dead servant, saw in it the man, his character and his actions. To most of us the skull is a death icon, drawing attention to something to be feared. Everyone recognises the skull and crossbones on the death's head hawk moth. But ask yourself what that image means to you. Mortal danger as on a bottle of a poisonous substance or by a high voltage power line? Pliny, no doubt using the simple logic of the lawyer that he was, is said to have used a mare's skull in an attempt to repel butterflies from his garden. Every child of my generation in England was brought up on a diet of stories of pirates and adventures on the high seas, such as Robert Louis Stevenson's *Treasure Island*, a tradition that is revived now and again in a new Hollywood movie. The sudden hoisting of the Jolly Roger with a white skull and crossbones traced on a black background was the pirate's battle flag, designed to strike terror into the hearts of potential victims by its very presence. The origins of this symbol are not easy to trace and are no doubt multiple. Some hold to the theory that 'Jolly Roger' is a corruption of '*La Jolie Rouge*', the latter being the red flag that was used first by English Privateers by order of the Admiralty in 1694 and which signified, by the obvious association with blood, that no life would be spared in battle. It was subsequently retained by some pirates as a device even more threatening than the dreaded black Jolly Roger.

The first German submarines were regarded as "damned un-English" by the Royal Navy and their crews were considered pirates.[i] As a result the Jolly Roger was flown by a British submarine in the First World War after sinking German ships. The Jolly Roger is today the emblem of the Royal Navy Submarine Service, and was flown by HMS *Conqueror* returning from the Falklands after her infamous sinking of the *Belgrano*. More recently, HMS *Trafalgar* returned to Plymouth in 1992 flying the Jolly Roger: it was later revealed that she was the first Royal Navy ship to fire Tomahawk cruise missiles in the Afghanistan war.

Skulls have had a great significance since Neolithic times in old Europe.[ii] A seven thousand year-old burial found in Lower Saxony has the skull of a young child in an egg-shaped pot. It seems likely that such tombs were equivalent to a desperate prayer for rebirth of young children or new-born babies. The skull was sprinkled with red ochre, the colour of blood, which was needed for reincarnation. This symbolic burial speaks to us over the millennia as

an expression of grief tempered by hope and faith, expressing much the same emotions as Michelangelo's sublime *Pietà*.

According to St John,[iii] Christ carried his own cross to the Place of the Skull, which was known in Aramaic as *Golgotha*. This may have given emphasis to the significance of the skull in Christian symbolism. In the Middle Ages the skull and crossbones was the battle flag of the Knights Templar, formed in 1118. Some historians believe that the Templars moved to Scotland when they were defeated in France in 1307, and their gravestones from then on were marked with the skull and crossbones. Gradually, the same motif was woven into the ceremonies of Freemasonry as a symbol of mortality and freedom from the physical world.

In medieval times, the skull was a symbol of death throughout Western Europe. Saints such as St Francis of Assisi were often painted in prayer or contemplation with a skull in one hand. The saying developed in seventeenth-century Italy E*t in Arcadia ego* meant 'even in Arcadia (the land of eternal pleasure) I (death) am present.' This became the theme of paintings by Guercino and others, finally adopted by Nicolas Poussin, in his eponymous painting in which three shepherds in the countryside examine fallen masonry which bears the Latin inscription and which in his first picture has a skull resting on it. Poussin omitted the skull in the second version of his painting known as *Les Bergers d'Arcadie* and death was then represented by a shepherdess resting her hand on the shoulder of one of the shepherds. Poussin's painting, incidentally, has attracted considerable attention in recent years because claims were made that it depicts the village of Rennes-le-Château in the background and the painting was interpreted as a document showing in a complex coded form where the Holy Grail – supposedly taken to the church by the Cathars – might be situated.

Artists often placed a skull in their portraits as an allusion to the impermanence of existence: the so-called 'Vanitas' symbol (Vanitas meaning 'emptiness' in Latin). One example is in *The Ambassadors* by Hans Holbein, which is perhaps the most famous picture in the National Gallery in London. This magnificent portrait of two wealthy men, surrounded by the trappings of their learning, travels and influence over the world, has in the foreground a whitish-grey streak of paint which is an anamorphic death's head, that is, when viewed in a mirror or from a particular angle, for example from the side, it becomes a grinning skull. It is likely that the painting was intended to be hung near a doorway, so that people walking past would suddenly see the skull image appear in front of them as a reminder of death lurking everywhere and of the impermanence of existence. A crucifix is hidden in a corner of the picture, perhaps as a symbol of protection.

left: **Skull from burial, Kamora, Crete; Greek and Roman period (300-200 BC). The gold wreath suggests an athlete, and a coin for the ferryman is alongside. Agios Nikolaos Archaeological Museum**

right: **Pot burial of child from Crete (Krya). Late Minoan period (1400-1300 BC). Agios Nikolaos Archaeological Museum**

The Ambassadors by Hans Holbein, showing the anamorphic skull in the foreground

This picture was painted at the time of the bubonic plague, which was to kill Holbein ten years later in 1543, so death was tapping on the shoulders of everyone at that time.

Skulls figured in the lives of the Aztec and Mayan cultures of Central America – not surprising given the immense quantities generated by ritual sacrifice. The skull signified death, which prepared for resurrection of the spirit and for the reappearance of the sun in the morning. Some temples were flanked by skull-racks containing the skulls of prisoners taken in battle, and others who had the privilege of being chosen for an early trip to join the gods. On ceremonial occasions tens of thousands of sacrifices are said to have been made by the Aztecs. The skulls of the dead were arranged on special skull racks in front of the temples or pyramids where the sacrifices had taken place and appear to have served as icons. This practice appears to have survived in the intervening centuries in a less sanguineous form to the present-day as the ceremony of the *Día de los Muertos* (Day of the Dead) in Mexico during which it is believed that the dead souls revisit their families, and representations of skulls become personal icons for the relatives of a dead person.

Skulls also feature in the architecture of Mayan temples, and there are curious accounts of glass skulls that have survived the Spanish conquest of Central America. In *The Mystery of the Crystal Skulls* Chris Morton and Ceri Louise Thomas give an account of their investigations into

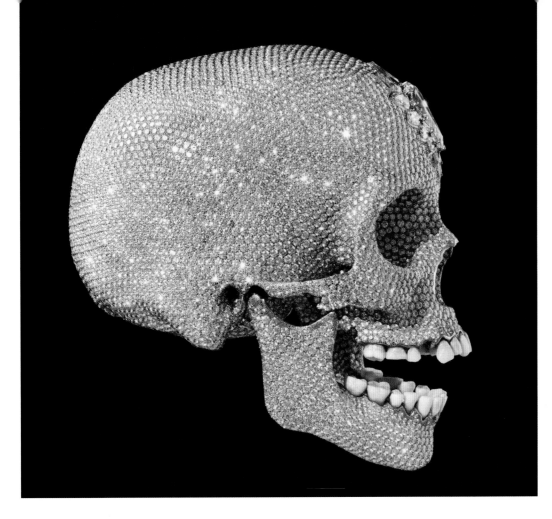

left: **Damien Hirst's sculpture *For the Love of God* presenting a symbolic and cynical view of the *mores* of the Western world. Hirst claims to have sold it for £50 million**

below: **The crystal skull, reputedly made by the Aztecs, but considered now to be of more recent origin. This is said to be the inspiration for Damien Hirst's jewelled skull artwork**

an old Native American legend that thirteen crystal skulls were made which were said to be repositories of all the information necessary for the survival of the human race. They succeeded in locating several of these skulls, which had been produced with immense technical skill by artists whose techniques remain a great mystery.

The first skull known to the authors had been found by the British archaeologist Frederick Mitchell-Hedges in 1924 and was in the possession of his daughter Anna who explained that the skull was believed by the Maya to have great powers of healing, and was also used in a ritual transfer of knowledge and wisdom from a dying person to a young person. The account of Morton and Thomas leads us into aspects that are purely mythical and often highly tendentious, but it is nevertheless plain that the skulls were artefacts connected with the Mayan creation myth described in the *Popol Vuh*. This is the only surviving account of the religious beliefs and traditions of the Quiché Maya of Guatemala. A Dominican priest, Father Francisco Ximinez, who had learnt the Quiché language, fell upon the original manuscript buried beneath a church and translated it into Spanish in the middle of the sixteenth century. The original was then lost.

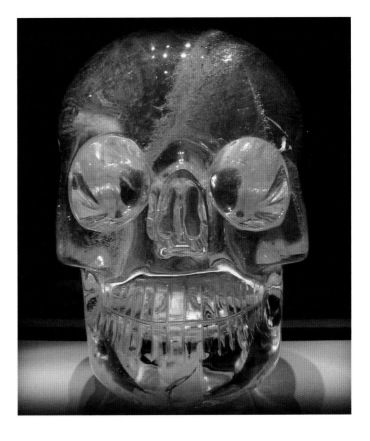

In the *Popol Vuh*, two of the Lords of the Underworld, Hun-Hunahpu and Vucub-Hunahpu are defeated by evil deities and the head of the former is put in a calabash tree, which immediately bears fruit. The tree is visited by a young girl, Xquic, who, like Eve in the Garden of Eden, fears to pick the fruit.

A skull in the branches says, "What is it you wish? Those round objects which cover the branches of the trees are nothing but skulls." The skull of Hun-Hunahpu then tells her to reach for the skull with her right hand. As she does so, a few drops of saliva fall on her hand and disappear. The voice in the tree says,

"In my saliva and spittle I have given you my descendants. Now my head has nothing on it any more, it is a skull without flesh." The voice explains that the image of the lord, the wise man or the orator does not disappear, but is bequeathed to the daughters and the sons. Xquic finds she is pregnant and the two lords that are born to the virgin then become the Hero Twins of the Mayan cosmogony.

The devotion of the ancient Mexicans to skull icons has been seized on and elaborated by the contemporary British artist Damian Hirst, who has attracted immense publicity for his artwork based on a skull. Entitled *For the Love of God* and valued at £50 million, this skull has been encrusted with 8,601 diamonds set in platinum. The aim of the artist was to raise questions about the way we live and the values we have. Critics referred to the magnetic attraction of the image when it was first put on display in London in June 2007, but the artwork draws our attention to the morality of using art as a symbol or alternative to wealth, and invites a comparison with the wealth wasted and the life and the beauty destroyed in death and war.

The Romans laid out skeletons in catacombs, preserving mainly the skull and long bones which were the most resistant to decay. Eventually, the stone carvings were instituted at the entrances to graveyards and catacombs, serving as a *Memento Mori* – a reminder reflected in the Christian service of Committal ('In the midst of life we are in death…').

Among the awe-inspiring mosaics that have been recovered from Pompeii is one from a *triclinium* (the dining area of a house), which shows a symbolic view of existence. A skull (*memento mori*) rests on a butterfly (representing the liberated soul), which in turn is resting on the wheel of time, or perhaps the wheel of fortune, capable of turning one way or the other. Suspended from a level on each side of the skull are two robes, one the purple robe of an important and wealthy person entwined around a sceptre, and one of a beggar, with his sackcloth, both brought to the same level in death. The butterfly has a mixture of colours including purple, brown and white, which were used in clothing to signify rank and status. It may be an illustration of the lesser purple emperor butterfly, *Apatura ilia*, which has those colours as well as eye spots on each wing, and which must have been regarded as a noble insect because of its purple colour, revered by the Romans.

By combining the sobering reminder of our own mortality with ancient beliefs about rebirth, the chrysalis or pupal stage came to symbolise death in Christian teachings, and

Detail from Gisleni's tomb in the church of Santa Maria del Popolo in Rome. The silk moth, representing the soul, is reborn from the chrysalis in the cocoon

emergence from the pupa represented rebirth, so the life of Christ has been equated with the growth and metamorphosis of a butterfly. The skull image has been associated with this. In early Christian art, the ascent of the soul at death was frequently represented as a butterfly escaping from a chrysalis.

This metaphor is illustrated in the church of Santa Maria del Popolo in Rome, where the architect, Gisleni, constructed his own marble epitaph in 1670, two years before he died. His tomb bears two plaques set in a marble plinth, one with a caterpillar spinning a chrysalis around it, and the other with a moth emerging from the cocoon and flying away, with the inscription, "Neither alive in this world or dead in the next." The two plaques are directly above a skeleton in a shroud, imprisoned in a cage that suggests the moth incarcerated in the cocoon, while at the top of the plinth a kind of *trompe l'oeil* portrait of the artist in his prime marks his rebirth.

In the mid-eighteenth century, the skull and crossbones was used as military insignia (the *Totenkopf* or death's head symbol) on uniforms in the Hussar regiment under Frederick the Great. In the Napoleonic wars the Brunswick armed forces changed their uniforms to black with a *Totenkopf* badge in mourning for their leader, Frederick, Duke of Brunswick-Luneburg, after he was killed in battle.

More recently, the skull and crossbones emblem was adopted by Hitler's bodyguard, the *Stabwache*, which later became the SS. The head of the SS was Theodor Eicke, who had played a major role in the infamous Night of the Long Knives, and who then became responsible for setting up units known as the *Totenkopfverbände* (Death's Head Units) controlling the running of the concentration camps. The Nazi SS officers used the skull and crossbones on their uniform caps, and on a ring – the highly prized *Totenkopfring* – which initially was presented to officers for their leadership in battle and loyalty to the Nazi regime. Eventually, in the Second World

War the ring was available to all officers of the SS, including the Gestapo. The ring was designed for Himmler, and apart from the skull, which derived from use in the old Prussian armies, featured lightning flashes (symbolising victory), various runes representing faith and camaraderie, and the swastika.

At the end of the war, Himmler regarded the rings as token insignia of his own personal philosophy, and ordered all rings to be sent back to him when the owner died. They were all collected in Wewelsburg castle in Rhine-Westphalia and sealed into rock nearby. About 3,500 rings are believed to be in existence today, and one has recently been offered on eBay as a collectors' item for ten thousand US dollars.

Wewelsburg is said to be the sacred castle of the SS where Himmler indulged his own perverted mythological fantasies. It appears that he intended to establish the castle as the centre of a new empire cast in the Nazi mode and set to last for the next millennium. Perhaps inspired by the legend of King Arthur and Camelot, he constructed a room with a round table and with the coat of arms of the leading SS officers around the walls. The table looked down on a black sun in the floor, and this symbol has been adopted by some neo-Nazis as an alternative to the (banned) swastika.

The historical perspective shows us that the skull is a powerful affective symbol that has found a variety of meanings. But with any symbol the meaning that is ascribed to it depends on the context in which it is placed and on the associations that the observer makes in his or her mind. As we have seen, the skull served in earlier times as a symbol of regeneration, as a *memento mori*, as an icon of the dead, as a military insignia, as a potent threat, a signal of impending attack, a psychological weapon, a representation of deities, a warning of mortality, an emblem of power...

In addition to the ancient symbol of the skull, the Nazis took over the swastika, thus giving them both new meaning, tainting them in our minds today with associations of horror and crimes that that regime perpetrated. In the Nazi regime, the swastika completely lost the autochthonous meaning it had held for millennia in the Far East. For the Nazis it was an emblem of the Aryan race, but for the rest of the Western world it has remained a symbol of evil.

In 2005, Prince Harry, the third in line to the throne of England, created a furore when he arrived at a fancy dress party sporting a swastika armband. The media had a field day, and immediately members of the European parliament called for a Europe-wide ban on the symbol, which has come to signify hate, death, murder and anti-Semitism. Although there are examples of the swastika symbol going back ten thousand years, it was only when a German archaeologist, Heinrich Schliemann (ironically a Jew) found pottery with the swastika design in excavations of Troy and Mycenae that the symbol was appropriated by the Nazi party because of its assumed association with the Aryan race.

After the publicity, there was an immediate backlash from the Hindus in Britain for whom the swastika has a totally different significance. The name is derived from the Sanskrit word *svastika*, which has been interpreted as 'Let good prevail.' This symbol is widely used on buildings as a kind of good luck charm. For this meaning, the arms must bend to the right (the form adopted by the Nazi party). The version with arms turned to the left signifies death in Hindu mythology. Hindus in Britain expressed dismay at the way in which a symbol depicting the wheel of life and good fortune had become a symbol of racism, torture and war.[iv]

These two symbols, the skull and the swastika, have wielded remarkable power over the emotions of millions of people. That is the way a symbol seems to work, by acting as key to unlock a box containing a host of feelings and associations. Sometimes it is a Pandora's box, sometimes not, depending on our culture and experience. The famous psychologist C.G. Jung collected information about such symbols and showed that they coincided with deep-rooted configurations in the human psyche, which he termed *archetypes*. But whether or not archetypes exist (I shall argue later that they do), the fact remains that the meaning or interpretation of symbols rests on what we have learnt for ourselves about the context in which those symbols are used. This notion applies to the death's head marking on the eponymous moth with which this chapter began. This marking may affect different people in different ways. How then, do the hawk moth's enemies – birds, reptiles and insectivores – perceive the symbol? If it does not mean the same to all humans, how can we presume to know how animals see it?

The Looking Glass

"'He's dreaming now,' said Tweedledee: 'and what do you think he's dreaming about?'

Alice said 'Nobody can guess that.'

'Why, about you!' Tweedledee exclaimed, clapping his hands triumphantly. 'And if he left off dreaming about you, where do you suppose you'd be?'

'Where I am now, of course,' said Alice.

'Not you!' Tweedledee retorted contemptuously. 'You'd be nowhere. Why, you're only a sort of thing in his dream!'

'If that there King was to wake,' added Tweedledum, 'you'd go out— bang!—just like a candle!'"

Lewis Carroll: *Through the Looking Glass*

L ewis Carroll, in the dialogue between Alice and Tweedledum and Tweedledee, was making a point about the nature of reality – one that the philosopher Bertrand Russell described as 'painful' if you fully understand it. Does anything exist except as a representation in our minds? This leads on to the question of whether that representation, in whatever form it is, is a 'true' form of reality or a transformed image of what is real.

The camera, it is said, cannot lie, but by manipulation of the image during development and printing it can give rise to something false. Similarly, the visual image produced in the brain – what we perceive – can be a lie. The eye is not even a good optical instrument: it produces an imperfect, inverted, image on the retina. Helmholtz, who was one of the first to investigate its functioning in the late nineteenth century, wrote:

> "Now it is not too much to say that if an optician wanted to sell me an instrument which had all these defects, I should think myself quite justified in blaming his carelessness in the strongest terms, and giving him back his instrument. … All these imperfections would be exceedingly troublesome in an artificial camera and in the photographic picture it produced."

Helmholtz's work was the first recognition that the image that falls on the retina is distorted reality, which is then 'corrected', as he put it, to eliminate the distortions. This is part of the process that we understand as 'perception'.

We all know, but tend to forget, that the brain can generate its own images, as in dreams, hallucinations induced by drugs, intense meditation, or illness. Anyone who has suffered, as I do, from migraine, will have been alarmed the first time that bright pulsed lights and lines with jagged edges came into their vision. This is caused by imbalances in the blood flow to the visual cortex. A relative of mine with secondary cancer in the brain really did 'see' hundreds of flies on the walls of the hospital ward. We need no further evidence that what we see with the eye is transformed by the incredible computing power of nerve cells to the dynamic three-dimensional picture that we call 'reality'.

Understanding perception contributes to an understanding of consciousness, but both these phenomena are scarcely better understood than they were at the time of Plato and Aristotle. Many of today's philosophers see reality as 'represented' in the mind, and divide the process of visual perception into two processes. The first is called object perception and is analogous to production of an image on the screen of a digital camera. The second is fact perception, and this

previous page: **Sequential images of a butterfly in flight. Whatever the point of view and change in attitude of the wings we are still convinced we are seeing the same butterfly, and it is a large white like the one inset**

above: **The large white butterfly (*Pieris brassicae*) at rest: an image that we instantly recall from memory after a glimpse of the insect in flight**

is the process in which the image is given meaning. To carry the analogy further, we know that computers can be programmed to interpret images produced by a camera, by matching stored images with the incoming one and so interpreting and classifying it. An example is the use of patterns in the iris for recognising individuals. The camera that photographs the iris 'sees' an image, which has no connotations until it is compared with stored images. Then, if a match is found this confirms the identity of an individual.

The brain is believed to do something similar. This must involve each person forming a model in the mind built up as a result of experience and background knowledge, which allows an object to be recognised as, say, a cat, independently of perspective, lighting, colour, posture, point of view, or movement of the cat. This is a tremendous feat, infinitely more complicated than recognising the colour patterns on the iris. It is not surprising that we make mistakes in interpreting the sensory data that the eye records and passes to the visual cortex of the brain as a pattern of nerve impulses. Such errors can then be the cause of illusions: a black scarf on the sofa might for a brief moment be recognised as a cat; Superman could be mistaken for a plane; and, closer to the argument I am developing, a moth can be mistaken for a bat, and a fly for a wasp.

Star clusters and clouds create illusions. Shakespeare's *Hamlet* highlights this in a dialogue between Polonius and Hamlet, in which they agree that a particular cloud is like a camel, a weasel, or "very like a whale".

Again, in *Anthony and Cleopatra*, Shakespeare ponders on the same issue:

> *"Sometimes we see a cloud that's dragonish;*
> *A vapour sometime like a bear or lion,*
> *A tower'd citadel, a pendant rock,*
> *A forked mountain or blue promontory*
> *With trees upon't, that nod unto the world*
> *And mock our eyes with air : ..."*

In a stimulating essay on "The Image in the Clouds" E.H. Gombrich[i] shows how projection of an artist's inner visions onto clouds has given rise to invention. Leonardo da Vinci advocated the use of such diffuse images to stimulate the mind and suggest new possibilities to artists. Botticelli, according to Leonardo, had said that in throwing a sponge full of paint at the wall a blot is left where one sees a fine landscape. It remains to be said that Leonardo was unimpressed by his fellow artist's landscapes.

Disturbance to the brain through the medium of drugs can then radically alter perception, and provide us with a different 'reality', as Aldous Huxley described in *The Gates of Perception* and *Heaven and Hell* after taking mescaline. Damage to certain parts of the brain can also cripple perception, of the kind that Oliver Sacks wrote about in his book *The Man Who Mistook His Wife for a Hat*. The man in question had an impaired ability to recall complex images and could distinguish his wife most easily from other figures by the green hat that she wore.

Perception is without doubt an immensely complicated process, and we can infer that each template (in whatever form it exists) in the brain has a multitude of facets. The brain is able to compensate for changes in colour, brightness, shape and perspective that we experience continuously as our angle of vision changes, as the light reflected from objects changes in intensity and wavelength, and as objects are seen against different background colours. Without our amazing ability to maintain an image of a stable world, Gombrich argues, art could not exist.

In what we see, we maintain what is termed 'size constancy'. This means, for example, that when you take your dog for a walk, the dog will appear to you to stay the same size as it runs towards you or away from you, whether the image fills the retina or just a tiny part of it. If you make the dog sit, and then walk around it in a circle, it will continue to be the same dog although your point of view changes, and the outline of the dog with it. Not only that, but your golden retriever, or whatever it happens to be, will stay the some colour in full sunlight, in the shade, or under street lights, even though the reflected light from its coat changes because the spectrum of light falling on it in those different light conditions differs markedly. This amazing computational ability is known as 'colour constancy'.

top: **Storks are commonly seen nesting on roofs in Crete**

bottom: **The storks on closer inspection reveal themselves as chimney cowls. The elementary features of the long neck and the head with a beak easily deceive our interpretation from a distance**

Electrophysiological recordings from the visual nervous pathways in the brains of animals, together with the results of simple experiments on animal behaviour, help us to understand how sense data are analysed. Animals with brains of relatively low complexity – insects, amphibians, reptiles and birds – generally rely more on the array of nerve cells forming a felt at the back of the light-sensitive cells (rods and cones in the case of vertebrates) to detect certain features of the image, rather than using the brain to do so. Most mammals, on the other hand, rely more upon the visual cortex of the brain to interpret the patterns of light falling on the retina, an issue that will be examined more closely later. This places all the demands on the brain but allows judgments to be made on the basis of previous experience and context.

A simple analogy would be a cold store equipped with fire alarms, temperature sensors, voltage meters and intruder alarms. Any one of these going off signals an emergency and dictates pre-determined remedial action, which the security officer initiates. However, the fire alarm may be set off by smoke from someone's cigarette, the intruder alarm by a spider, and the temperature sensor and the voltmeter may have a poor electrical contact that gives false readings. The security officer might therefore choose to respond in quite a different way if he has video cameras to show him everything in the building; then all of the circumstances can be taken into account before appropriate action is taken, but the officer has to rely on previous experience, instructions and knowledge in his or her decision-making.

In a mountain village in Crete, I was not surprised to see that some of the chimney stacks on the stone houses were occupied by nesting storks – I had seen them in other parts of Europe dominating the roof-tops. But it was a day or two before the penny dropped: these were not storks but chimney cowls, fulfilling the dual function of helping the up-draught through the chimneys and signalling to storks that the suitable nesting sites were already taken. The basic features of a long neck and the head with a long beak were alone sufficient elements to conjure up the far more complex image of a real stork in my mind. Animals have a similar ability to respond to simple elements of a visual pattern, although this may depend much less on memory than it does in us, and this phenomenon is vital to understanding the evolution of wing patterns in insects.

When I entered University in the late 1950s, Konrad Lorenz's delightful book *King Solomon's Ring*, written for a popular audience, was recommended reading, and marked the beginning of the science of ethology: the scientific study of animal behaviour. Lorenz wrote engagingly about the animals he lived with, who had become like mutual friends, and found that they responded to each other, and to certain other objects, including threats to themselves, with stereotyped and easily recognised behaviour patterns or displays, which he regarded as instinctual. But their perception appeared to be different from ours in that they commonly responded to only part of what came into their visual field. A good example of this was seen in the responses of his hand-reared jackdaws. These birds treated him as one of their own kind, but one day he was attacked by a screeching bird. He quickly discerned that the cause of the attack was the black bathing trunks that he had been wearing and had brought out of his pocket. The birds had perceived this as a young jackdaw that had been captured, even though it was only something black with none of the features of symmetry and shape that we would rely upon as vital clues to its identity.

Many similar examples of aggression towards simple formless patches of colour came to light as zoologists left the laboratory and took to the field. In his book on the life of the robin, David Lack revealed the shocking truth about how vicious territorial males can be in defending their territory against other males, which they identify by the red breast. He found that a bunch of red feathers in a robin's territory was sufficient to provoke a fierce attack by the territory holder. Niko Tinbergen, who shared a Nobel Prize with Lorenz, made a study of sticklebacks, freshwater fish in which the males have a bright red abdomen. As a boy fishing in ponds with a net and a jam-jar I used to know them as 'robins'. He found that other males saw a simple disc of wood painted red below as a rival when it was put into the water. Even a red post-office van passing by appeared to alarm the fish. Curiously, at the time of writing this, there were reports in the media of a cock pheasant repeatedly pursuing a post-office van down a country lane in Devon and attacking it, presumably because the van was flaunting the red colour of the cock pheasants' plumage.

Tinbergen and his colleagues studied what Lorenz called 'releasers' of social behaviour in greater depth in animals ranging from hunting wasps to seagulls, and coined the term 'sign stimulus' for the abstracted features of an object that animals such as these could be shown to recognise and respond to. His work inspired a generation of zoologists at Oxford, where he became the first Professor of Animal Behaviour. One was Desmond Morris who went on to show that many aspects of human behaviour involved responses to just certain features of an object or another person, provoking automatic or 'instinctive' responses. This invites, incidentally, a comparison with Jungian archetypes and their associated symbols.

The response of the male stickleback or the robin to the quality of redness alone does not, however, tell us the whole story. Orientation of the model and the context in which it is presented are among other features that influence the responsiveness of such animals, so we are drawn towards the view of perception that sees it as a process of matching the information from the eyes (and other sense-organs usually) with a template, formed either in the brain, or, as we have seen, in the nerve cells of the retina. A very curious phenomenon is the tendency of animals to react most strongly of all to a stimulus that accentuates certain features (perhaps in a similar way to how we respond to the faces drawn by newspaper cartoonists). For example a herring gull chick pecks at a red spot on the base of the parent's bill, which is a signal for the adult to regurgitate food for the chick. Tinbergen[ii] and his fellow scientists found that a narrow rod with red and white bands was more effective as a target for the chick than a faithful model of the adult: it combines elongation, redness, and colour contrast. Stimuli like this are called 'super-stimuli', and Desmond Morris was quick to point out in his best-selling book *The Naked Ape* that super-stimuli, for example in a woman's over-developed breasts, lips and buttocks, can be shown to influence human sexual behaviour (and thereby, perhaps for some men, choice of daily newspaper).

The dependence of perception on certain key features was then shown to be something that was not just common to birds and mammals, but was a general rule throughout the animal kingdom. Tinbergen showed, again using simple experiments with models, that insects respond only to particular features of a visual image. The grayling butterfly, which is common on heathland in northern Europe, has a complex courtship ritual, which begins with the male flying up from its resting place to accost a female that comes flying along. Tinbergen tied butterfly models of

A herring gull (*Larus argentatus*). The red spot on the yellow bill is the target for begging pecks of the young gull chicks. But the chick sees only red, colour contrast, and something long and thin. A stick with red and yellow rings painted on it is even more attractive than the real bill

various colour patterns, shape and size to a fishing line, and found that the butterflies did not pay much attention to the colour, wing-patterns and shape of the model, although they preferred black or red female models over the actual brown and yellow females. Shape was not important – even a rectangle would do – and larger models were preferred to models of the natural size. The overriding feature was the dancing movement achieved by shaking the model as it was flown through the air.

The existence of super-stimuli, though, is of great importance for the understanding of what is reality for animals. First, it suggests that the models or templates in the brains of animals against which visual images are matched are relatively crude, so that it is easy for an animal to misinterpret what its senses are telling it. Secondly, and very importantly for understanding what goes on in mimicry, it suggests that the mimic of another animal does not have to look exactly like the real thing to obtain benefit from the resemblance. This point will be taken up again in coming chapters. Thirdly, it provides a possible explanation for repeated designs on the wings of butterflies and moths; for example, we see not just one pair of eye-spots, resembling a bird's eye, on the wings of many brown butterflies, and on the undersides in some nymphalid butterflies, but a series of eye-spots.

In the 1970s, a group of engineers and biologists from the Massachusetts Institute of Technology[iii] wrote a paper entitled "What the frog's eye tells the frog's brain". To answer this question they tapped into the nervous traffic travelling between the retina of the eye and the brain. They found that the frog's eye was mostly unresponsive to images of its normal environment of reeds, water and banks projected onto a screen, but if a fly-sized black dot was moved across the screen certain nerve cells burst into action. If a duck-sized shadow was moved into view then another group of nerve cells shot off their coded message to the brain. Continuing, they found a number of detectors in the deeper layers of the retina that are analogous to the pattern

recognition devices of computer software programmes, each type cued to respond to a specific feature or group of features. So the frog's eye has detectors for bugs, predators (herons perhaps), water, and twilight. The frog's brain has relatively little to do in terms of analysis of images falling on the retina; perception is a sorting-out and classifying process, which is, to use the ungainly computer jargon, 'hard-wired'.

Similar studies were made on the brains of cats: unlike frogs, the cat's eye itself appears to carry out relatively little analysis, and that takes place mainly in the visual cortex of the brain. Hubel and Wiesel achieved fame for their identification of 'classifying cells' in the visual cortex, which are pre-programmed to respond, for example, to the orientation of lines and outlines, so that specific cells are triggered by a line projected onto the retina at a particular angle to the vertical, or with a particular degree of curvature. It seems to follow that exaggeration of the salient features of a visual image that are analysed by a number of different neural detectors will tend to reduce ambiguity to a minimum, and so explain why a super-stimulus is so potent. If our brain works similarly, this may be one reason why circles and squares have become attributes of Jungian archetypes – attributes of the unconscious with which we are born, and it may also explain the lines and dazzling circles of a migraine attack that result from the classifying cells being somehow stimulated into activity.

The recurrence of the colour red as a 'releaser' of animal behaviour may not be coincidental. Red is used by us in all kinds of signals, usually signifying danger (as in traffic control, warning notices, red alerts) or to draw attention to something (overdue bills, military uniforms in former times, red carpets, red lights in brothels, etc.). In an analysis of ninety-eight languages categorising the words for different colours ranging in eleven different spectral colours, Berlin and Kay[iv] found that some languages recognised only black and white, but the next most common was red, followed by yellow and green.

The use of red ochre has been traced as far back as the Upper Palaeolithic (over 12 000 to 32 000 BC). Leroi-Gourhan regards red as the symbol of blood and life in this era, where "the separation of the physical, the magical and the aesthetic is impossible". Neolithic and Palaeolithic cave art made use principally of red ochre and black colorants. The selection of these colours appears to have been deliberate because other colours were available, including yellow (which was rarely used), and because their preparation was quite a sophisticated process. By twelve to thirteen thousand years ago, pigments were being prepared from materials that came from different sites: haematite (red) and manganese dioxide (black), mixed together with extenders. In the Lascaux caves the black pigment is 15 per cent manganese dioxide, and the colorant 25 per cent ground quartz and 40 per cent calcium phosphate. The calcium phosphate was produced by heating bone to 400°C and then grinding it. Clearly, then, the choice of colour was a deliberate process influenced by preconception and prepared according to a formula.

Seventy-five pieces of ochre and ochre-stained grindstone were found in the Kapthurin Formation in South Africa, and dated to around 280 000 BC.[v] Red, then, has had meaning and symbolic importance for almost the whole of human history of which traces remain. It is the colour of blood, and therefore originally was associated with birth, death (by wounding), and because of that, possibly, the sun at the beginning and the end of the day. Pliny[vi] wrote of the phantasmagorical basilisk: "Its blood the magi praise to the skies, telling how it thickens as does pitch, and resembles pitch in colour, but becomes brighter red than cinnabar when diluted." Many other meanings and associations have been added to these by the cultures in which we now live.

At twilight, particularly in the tropics and sub-tropics, the colours of vegetation seem to be enhanced, particularly the greens and blues, while reds become darker and darker. John Barrow[vii] suggests that this is because at sundown the yellow and green components of light from the sun are absorbed in the upper atmospheric layers, so light is more intense in the blue-violet and red zones. If the eye were equally sensitive to all colours in the visible spectrum we would then see red flowers and blue flowers standing out bright at dusk against the green vegetation. However, the eye responds mainly to blue and green, and, curiously, shifts its sensitivity at night becoming less sensitive to red and more sensitive to blue. This means that we have heightened sensitivity to the blue-green end of the spectrum at dusk, while red colours, including the night

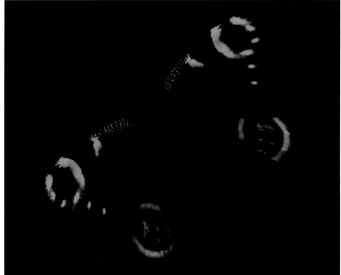

sky, remain dark. Colour constancy is sacrificed for the enhancement of brightness of other colours against a reddish background. It is interesting that the large eye-spots of many nocturnal moths have a bluish colouring to the 'pupil' which makes them more visible in dim light. The same applies to the eye-spots of the peacock butterfly, which, although it is not nocturnal, hibernates in dark places such as hollow trees and displays its 'eyes' as a defence when disturbed.

It is humbling to think that, although we know how the eye and the brain sort the different wavelengths of light into categories, we have not the slightest idea of what sensation is and how it derives from neural activity: what is the greenness of green and the redness of red, and whether it is the same to you as it is to me.

We can discriminate easily between what we see as red, green, yellow, blue and violet, orange, pink and brown, and we can also distinguish thousands of different hues. Furthermore, the brain categorises black, white and grey – the so-called achromatic colours. Colours in these eight main categories are detected most easily, and also remembered most accurately, if the wavelength is in the middle of the category: the reddest red and the bluest blue are the most easily detected and recognised.

Human colour vision is referred to as 'trichromatic'. What this means is that the cone cells in the retina that mediate colour vision are tuned to pick up certain bands of colour, centred on red, blue and green (the primary colours). It is believed that trichromatic colour vision arose about forty million years ago, in the mammals that were ancestors of the primates. This would have helped them to find coloured fruits in the environment of forests when they moved from the savannas and other dry areas where little edible fruit exists. Many animals, including monkeys, tamarinds, reptiles, pigeons, goldfish and bees also have colour vision based on the same principles as our colour vision,[viii] but sometimes with important differences, the main one being high sensitivity to violet and ultraviolet light in many insects and birds.

It is likely, then, that the main predators of butterflies and moths can resolve the different colour patterns on a wing, but there is considerable evidence that they resolve more detail of colour and design than we do, as we shall see in a later chapter.

No aspect of perception can be explained, except in very simplistic terms, by analogy to the action of video cameras. Colin Blakemore changed our view of the recognition process when he compared the behaviour of kittens reared for the first few months of their life in surroundings in which they could see only vertical black and white stripes, with kittens that could see only horizontal stripes. When, at the end of this developmental period, they were put into a room with objects such as tables and chairs, there was an astonishing difference in the behaviour of the two groups. Kittens reared with horizontal stripes bumped into table legs. Those reared with vertical stripes did not do that, but would not play with a stick that was held horizontally; they behaved as if they could not see it. Blakemore then showed that the latter had scarcely any

Blue-tinted eye-spots of the peacock butterfly (*Inachis io*) as they would appear in very dim light. The blue-green shift has been simulated in these photographs

classifying cells for horizontal lines, and the former very few for vertical lines. Clearly, the development of the analytical apparatus of the visual cortex had been influenced by experience, and become moulded to fit the world the kittens saw.

The evidence that perception is shaped by experience very early on in life was soon confirmed by experiments on gulls, ducks and many other animals, putting paid to the dogma preached by the early ethologists who maintained that the automatic and stereotyped responses that animals produced were instinctive, by which they meant genetically inherited. A discussion of the great importance of early experience in human behaviour is way beyond the scope of this book, but it has been claimed that the art of tribal societies is influenced by the structure of the built environment in which children live, so the geometry and perspective of the visual art of autochthonous North American peoples who live in wigwams tends to differ from that of peoples brought up in cities.

It is not too difficult to arrive at the conclusion that our visual perception and that of most birds, reptiles and mammals, is, for want of a better word, programmed to cope with the particular visual world in which we, or they, habitually live. Most of us are no longer born and live in close contact with nature, and from an early age objects that do not occur in nature are part of our everyday lives, and colours and shapes acquire a symbolism that is different from that of our remote ancestors. A young child is surrounded by all kinds of toys and other objects, so that colour loses the meanings it formerly had. The child may drink from a red cup, a blue one, or any colour, see its mother wearing red lipstick, and father a red shirt, and the meaning of red then becomes confused, and the child has to learn to associate it with context. A small red sphere might initially be perceived as a ripe berry to the member of a remote Amazonian tribe, and to a bird or a monkey, but to you or me it is a bead of a necklace.

It follows from what I have just said that it is very easy for us to jump to conclusions about the nature of an object. The humming bird hawk moth, for example, has been known by that name since the eighteenth century, and because of its flight and the humming noise it produces while hovering it has frequently been mistaken for a humming bird. This is in spite of the fact that the moth is common in Asia, Africa and Europe, where there are no humming birds. The high wing-beat frequency though, is a necessity for hovering flight while feeding. The defence of this moth actually depends not on its likeness to a bird, but to a bumble-bee. The end of the abdomen, viewed from behind while the insect is feeding, resembles the body of a bumble-bee.

Plato, in his allegory of the prisoners, which he used to explain the process of enlightenment, pictured the way in which perception develops as a result of experience. He envisaged prisoners in a cave, who could see only shadows on the walls of the caves, cast by people with marionettes moving in front of the light from a fire. Plato then imagined what it would be like for one of the prisoners to be brought out of the cave into the light of the sun. His perception would obviously change as he became accustomed to the light, and, with that would come the awareness of true reality, self, cause and effect, and the desire to organise the new world around him. He would be changed forever and would know that what he saw in the cave was illusory.

This allegory was devised to portray the value of education and experience for the rulers of Plato's *Republic*, but as Iris Murdoch pointed out[ix] the 'cave' has become television, which presents us with "vivid scrappy images and disconnected oddments of information as insights into truth". We are liable to accept these, and so man tends to create his own reality for himself, and is happy to stay in the cave rather than undertake a spiritual journey from appearance to truth and enlightenment.

We can use the analogy of the cave to regard animals as the prisoners who see only the shadows of things, and ourselves as humans, the enlightened ones: those who live in an illuminated world in which there is a very different level of reality. We see an insect like the death's head hawk moth as a curious creature with a design on its thorax that has a symbolic significance for us, and many other apparent hieroglyphs on the wings of other species of moth and butterfly. It is certain that a bird or other animal sees only elementary shadows, but what do they mean to such creatures?

Beware of
the Snark

"…..To describe each particular batch:
Distinguishing those that have feathers, and bite,
And those that have whiskers, and scratch.
For although common Snarks do no manner of harm,
Yet I feel it my duty to say,
Some are Boojums"

Lewis Carroll: *The Hunting of the Snark: An Agony in Eight Fits*

The mythical Snark in Lewis Carroll's surrealistic poem, with its peculiar habits of eating breakfast at five o'clock tea-time and carrying about bathing machines, is an elusive creature, but hunting it carries a grave risk. Some Snarks are Boojums, and whoever encounters a Boojum softly and suddenly vanishes away.

It has been argued that the poem is about lunacy and the death of Carroll's revered uncle, who was an inspector of asylums, at the hands of a lunatic.[i] Nevertheless the poem is an allegory about the probability of disaster, and the hazards of perception. It foreshadows in a remarkable way the well-known story of Schrödinger's cat.

The physicist Erwin Schrödinger used this puzzle to explain, and perhaps to ridicule, one of the great paradoxes of quantum physics: that light appears to exist simultaneously in particle form and as energy in a wave form. The cat is in a closed box, which also contains a flask of cyanide, a hammer, an atom of radioactive material and a detector of radioactive particles. There is a fifty per cent probability that the atom will decay during the limited period of the experiment, at which time it will activate the detector, which then releases the hammer, smashing the bottle and resulting in the death of the cat. The essence of this model is to show that the cat must be either alive or dead while it is in the box (it cannot be both), but its state can only be guessed at, and that guess is therefore describable only in terms of mathematical probability – but the mathematical logic differs from common logic in assuming that the cat is both dead and alive at the same time. The issue is only resolved on opening the box when the real state of the cat is revealed. Schroedinger went on to develop a unified theory in which it is assumed that light particles interact with matter to produce wave forms, so that testing for effects produced by particles shows them to be present, and testing for waves also shows them to be present.

We now know that many species of butterfly and moth are extremely poisonous, and the problem for insectivores is to determine which these are so that they can be avoided. While most butterflies flying around are Snarks, a few are Boojums.

On a visit to Marrakesh once, I bought a bag of almonds from the market. A small proportion of them were bitter, and I spat them out. These bitter almonds come from a variety of the almond tree and they contain cyanides that are liberated when the nuts are mixed with water. These do not usually affect us because even if we eat them the amount of poison in them is relatively small, but birds can be greatly affected. In 1955 the authorities in California[ii] received reports of hundreds of dead goldfinches in a residential area. It emerged that an estate of houses had

been built on an old almond orchard that had some bitter almond trees in it. Many undried nuts were lying around unharvested and these had killed the finches. Some almonds are Boojums.

Deadly poisons lurk everywhere in the plants around us. Death would come instantly from eating a single seed of a luxuriant castor oil plant (they contain ricin, one of the most potent poisons known), from eating a leaf of the brilliantly coloured oleanders, or the fruit of the thorn apple, Datura. Uncooked green potatoes or kidney beans torn from the ground can kill. Apple seeds, walnuts and uncooked cassava contain cyanides, and the toxins in some wild mushroom species could destroy your liver. In the country, threats lurk in the scorpions under stones, as the snake sunning itself on the rocks, or as a wasps' nest. Without accumulating a good knowledge of plants and animals anyone trying to survive in the wild could easily die of poisoning. Animals also have to learn which insects are edible and which are not.

We can safely assume that plants and animals evolved mechanical defences before chemical defences. Only at a more advanced stage in evolution would plants have evolved the complex biochemical pathways to make toxins that they could store in their tissues without harm to themselves. Following on from that, insects would have developed ways of overcoming the defences of poisonous plants and so extending their range of food plants. Those that could tolerate specific toxins in their bodies could then use them for their own defence against predators.

Plants in particular defend themselves with spines, thorns and barbs, which like the sword, spear and halberd, are visible threats as well as lethal weapons. Some of the most formidable spines are carried by plants of the Agave family. Agave ferox from the deserts of Central America has fleshy leaves rising 6-8 ft. from the ground tipped with pointed spines about 6 in. long with the hardness of metal. It is not conceivable that these evolved as a defence against animals that are alive today; they could have evolved only as deterrents to dinosaurs. If that is the case they have presumably retained their spines for around a hundred million years, during which period there has been no disadvantage to the plants in having a powerful deterrent at the ready.

Animals have likewise developed fearsome weapons: teeth, claws, and spines, not just the vertebrate carnivores and the likes of hedgehogs and porcupines, but also numerous invertebrates, including scorpions, spiders, centipedes, ants and beetles. Some swallowtail butterflies, including Eurytides and Graphium species, have black tapered lines on their wings that suggest spines, such as those on Agave leaves, some of which concatenate in two spine-like projections from the hind-wings. Such species, which are found mainly in the New World where they overlap in

opposite: *Agave ferox*, 6-8 ft tall and defended by sharp dagger-like spines up to 2 in. long

above left: **The swallowtail (*Papilio glaucus*) has spine-like images and scalloped wing borders like ridged Agave leaves and yellow and black banding that echoes wasp colours**

above right: **A swallowtail butterfly (*Graphium agetes*) replete with images of spines**

distribution with the Agaves and spiny cacti, thus combine the images of stout spines with the black-on-yellow emblems of wasps (yellow-jackets, as they are known in the USA).

The rhinoceros beetle and many of the large scarabid beetles (dung beetles and their relatives) have bodies with impressive armour plate and thick thorny projections that give them immunity from predation. The curved jaws of such creatures appear to be mimicked by the tail markings of some swallowtail butterflies. These are often associated with rows of eye-spots that together with the sickle-like jaws invoke the impression of some alien creature from a science fiction film. It is even possible that butterflies living today carry markings portraying the jaws and eyes of long-extinct animals, which have persisted over millennia like the seven-foot spears of the Agave plants, and startle us today.

One of the most complete butterfly fossils was found in the Florissant shales of Colorado, which were formed from volcanic ash about thirty-four million years ago. It was so well-preserved that it was possible to say that it had reddish-orange colouration, similar to some of its present-day descendants. Amazingly, it has clearly marked eye-spots on each hind-wing, each at the base of a spine-like tail, similar to that of the *Eurytides* swallowtail, giving it a false head with two curved jaws. Presumably, these were features of some spider-like creature or giant centipede.

The use of poisons has been a potent force in evolution, and those animals that have no poisons or other 'mechanical' defences, like powerful claws or teeth, tend to copy those that do; they are known as 'mimics', and mimesis is very common among butterflies and moths. Butterfly or moth mimics not only copy dangerous animals, but, as everyone has experienced, many species copy features of the environment in which they live – dead leaves, bark, thorns, bird-droppings, grass stems and so on, thus enabling them to escape the attentions of predators. This used to be known as 'protective colouration' but the preferred term nowadays is *crypsis*. The message on the diaphanous wings of such cryptic creatures is that there is no message. This is most clearly shown in the so-called 'glass-wing' butterflies of the New World Tropics, which have wings that are almost completely transparent; transparent enough to make them invisible in the dappled light of the forest.

Crypsis can be a form of camouflage, and the same principles are then in operation in the natural world that are employed by the military today to conceal people and structures.

opposite: **A rhinoceros beetle with a tank-like outer skeleton and formidable curved spines on the head that make it painfully inedible for most predators**

above left: **The swallowtail butterfly (*Iphiclides podalirius feisthamelii*) which has tails that look like spiny 'jaws'**

above right: **The butterfly *Prodryas persephone*: an image reconstructed from photographs of a 34 million year-old fossil and comparisons with present-day species belonging to the same family**

overleaf: **Glass-wing or Ithomiine butterflies (*Greta oto*) feeding**

Greta oto, which can be almost invisible in the dappled light of tropical forests

Apart from matching of colours and patterns to the immediate surroundings, lines are blurred or disrupted so that it is difficult for the eye to pick out the outline of the camouflaged object. During the First World War, naval ships were 'dazzle painted'. This involved painting large irregular zig-zag patterns on the sides of a ship so that recognisable features, like the bridge of a battleship, its funnels and gun turrets were obliterated by the brighter dominant dazzle bands. At the same time, the dark image of the ship against the sea lost its outline. This ruse, dependent upon the effect of a bright resplendent image being superimposed upon an inconspicuous camouflaged one was largely successful and probably succeeded in saving many lives by painting such a veil over the destroyers that were employed in protecting convoys of merchant shipping.

The genius behind the development of dazzle camouflage was Norman Wilkinson, a young lieutenant in the RNVR.[iii] After painstaking experimentation with models of merchant ships placed on a revolving table and viewed through a periscope, he came up with several important principles. First, the light parts of the pattern should be painted in two light colours, each with a distinctive tone. This increased the chances of the colour blending with the sky, and helped to distort the image of the ship when painted with dark grey or black zebra stripes. Secondly, the

Caterpillar of the viceroy
butterfly (*Basilarchia archippus*)
disguised as a bird dropping

most vulnerable parts of the ship: the bridge, the stern and the bow, should be covered by the design so that their outlines were not defined by the colour coming to a stop. This made it difficult for a submarine to determine the course of the ship. Thirdly, sloping lines, curves or stripes were the most effective means of breaking up the ship's outline.

We generally find that man's inventions are anticipated by nature: the equivalent of dazzle painting is seen in many butterflies and moths, and the same principles seem to apply. This is not surprising because there is a clear parallel between a submarine hunting a merchant ship and a bird hunting an insect. There are many examples of butterflies with bright coloured bands on their wings, including many swallowtails. Some have black lines on a white background, including *Idea* butterflies from South-East Asia. These species have a pattern of black marks and veins on their diaphanous white wings. These marks are continued over the vulnerable head and body, concealing them as camouflage stripes conceal the bridge of a warship. The Malaysian forest butterfly, *Parthenos sylvia*, has black bands that extend laterally across the wings and body, obscuring the outline of the body.

In many butterflies, lines on the wings direct the eye towards a false head at the tail end of the insect. The conclusion of most biologists has been that the false heads are lures to deflect the attentions of predators, so that pecks or bites are directed towards the tips of the hind-wings. This is not difficult to accept, especially as butterflies are often captured with beak marks around eyespots at the tail end, or with pieces of hind-wing missing, but it does not preclude the likelihood that the two 'heads' create confusion. Ken Preston-Mafham, a very experienced biologist, wrote of his confusion on seeing in Mexico a blue butterfly which had a false head with filamentous tails.[iv] At first he thought he was seeing two butterflies copulating in the normal tail-to-tail position. "I cannot remember any occasion", he wrote, "when I have gone so cross-eyed or been so puzzled…" It was only by approaching very closely that he was able to resolve the image.

The science of semiotics, which guided the massive growth of the communications industry, is concerned, among other things, with signal transmission and detection. We learn much from this that helps us to understand how butterflies and moths escape detection. A signal can be easily detected if it stands out against the background noise. 'Noise' in this sense can mean literally that, if the signal is sound or speech. We all know how background conversation interferes with hearing at a cocktail party, but the concept of noise applies to signals in any form or medium.

The banded peacock swallowtail
(*Papilio palinurus*). The green
stripes on a black background
provide good camouflage at
ground level in the forest

opposite, clockwise from left:
Idea leuconoe, from S.E. Asia. The black lines on the wing veins are continued over the body and head obscuring their outline, mirroring the dazzle-painting technique used in military camouflage

Detail of the markings of the head and thorax of *Idea leuconoe*

Parthenos sylvia from Malaysia. The black bars on the wings break up the outline of the body

left: A map-wing butterfly (*Cyrestis* sp.) with a false head combined with a wing pattern that gives the insect the semblance of a moth with the fore-wings folded back horizontally

above: **The long-banded silverline butterfly, the** *Cerberus* **of the insect world. Each hindwing has false eyes and two antennae, and the markings on the wings replicate the markings of the abdomen, so that the insect appears to have three heads visible from different perspectives**

opposite above: **The cracker butterfly (***Hamadryas feronia***) with a 'noisy' wing pattern**

opposite below: **The Queen of Spain fritillary (***Argynnis lathonia***) which, like most fritillaries, has repetitive black marks on its wings, similar to breast feather markings on some birds**

In vision, noise means anything that interferes with your view of something, for example, mist, reflected sunlight, or background colours and patterns. The so-called 'cracker' butterfly has a wing pattern that can be described as 'noisy'. There is so much detail and repetition in the pattern that it takes time for the eye to scan it. The insect also produces audible noise, as the name implies. Darwin was one of the first to document this when he went ashore in Brazil and described it in A Naturalist's Voyage around the World.

So an insect can avoid the eyes of predators by resting where the light intensity is low and the background on which it sits has a similar colour and pattern to its wings. On the other hand, the way of sending a 'strong message', to use the politicians' cliché, is to keep the noise as low as possible and increase the intensity of the signal relative to the noise (the signal to noise ratio). The metaphor then implies a message that you cannot mistake or avoid listening to.

Strong messages are sent by very poisonous insects, usually in the form of very bright and conspicuous colours. The technical term for this type of signalling is *aposematism*. Many members of the day-flying moths of the families Arctiidae (tiger moths) and Ctenuchidae are aposematic, often coloured in bright reds, yellows, and iridescent blues, with bands of strong colour on their bodies. In his poem St Agnes' Eve Keats refers to the tiger moth:

> "And diamonded with panes of quaint device, Innumerable of stains and splendid dyes, As are the tiger moth's deep-damask'd wings".

It is generally assumed that the bright colours are a message warning predators that it would be dangerous for them to attempt to capture the insects. The nocturnal tiger moths and their

relatives also send acoustic signals to advertise their presence to insectivorous bats. These signals, like the echolocation cries that bats use in navigation, are entirely ultrasonic. The moths have ears, and when they detect the calls of an approaching bat they signal back to it using the same ultrasonic frequencies and repetition patterns. This either interferes with the bats' echolocation system or mimics the calls of another bat, causing confusion, or sends a 'strong signal' advertising distasteful prey.

It is not uncommon to find that an insect, which is well concealed at rest, suddenly reveals, as part of its strategy of distraction, brightly coloured hind-wings that attract the attention of the eye and dissolve the original shape. It switches instantly from a very low signal to noise ratio to a very high one, thereby challenging all the constancy mechanisms of perception and creating shock in the same way that a conjuring trick confounds your expectations. The death's head hawk moth is one such insect. It has

cryptically coloured fore-wings the colour of dark tree bark on which it is liable to rest, but when it senses a potential predator it opens its fore-wings to expose the bright yellow underwings (see page 29). Many large-bodied moths do the same, including the eponymous red and yellow underwing moths and many species of hawk moth.

One of the world's largest and most spectacular butterflies, the golden birdwing butterfly, *Troides aeacus*, which is found in tropical forests in the Far East, has a very similar protective disguise to the death's head. It has no skull marking, but the fore-wings are very like the wings of a small bird. They are blackish, traced with white lines giving the appearance of feather patterns. This insect also has a brightly coloured yellow and black abdomen, which is normally concealed, but when the insect is molested it moves its forewings so that its waspish abdomen appears. If captured, the insect exposes its brilliant yellow hind-wings and flexes its abdomen making stinging movements.

Many stick insects, mantids and grasshoppers, in their strategy of distraction, suddenly reveal brightly coloured hind-wings that attract the attention of the eye so that the original shape disintegrates and the insect reappears as a transmogrified creature. There are few more striking examples than those found among mantids, where a mantis that may show great resemblance to a twig, leaf or piece of bark will suddenly change its apparent shape and colour to become a threatening phantom. Jean-Henri Fabre, known as the 'poet of science', wrote a vividly evocative description early in the last century on the defensive display of the European Praying Mantis:

> "You see before you, most unexpectedly, a sort of bogey-man or Jack-in-the-box. The wing-covers open and are turned back on either side, slantingly: the wings spread to their full extent and stand erect like parallel sails or like a huge heraldic crest towering over the back; the tip of the abdomen curls upwards like a crosier, rises and falls, relaxing with short jerks and a sort of sough, a 'Whoof! Whoof!' like that of a turkey-cock spreading his tail. It reminds one of the puffing of a startled adder. Planted defiantly on its four hindlegs, the insect holds its long bust almost upright. The murderous legs…. open wide, forming a cross… and revealing the arm-pits decorated with rows of beads and a black spot with a white dot in the centre. These two faint imitations of the eyes in a Peacock's tail, together with the dainty ivory beads, are warlike ornaments kept hidden at ordinary times. They are taken from the jewel-case only at the moment when we have to make ourselves brave and terrible for battle."

Fabre added that the effect produced by this rapid change is so abrupt and so threatening that not only the behaviour but even the sudden thought of it startled him, causing him to draw back

previous page: **The garden tiger moth (***Arctia caja***) which advertises its distastefulness with startlingly bright and contrasting colour patterns. The effect of the display is heightened by sudden opening of the fore-wings to reveal the dazzling hind-wing colours**

above: **The European praying mantis (***Mantis religiosa***) in the so-called 'spectral attitude'**

opposite above: **The giant birdwing butterfly (***Troides aeacus***)**

opposite below: **The birdwing *Troides helena* with the bright yellow and black abdomen and hind-wings displayed to reveal what appears to be part of a large wasp**

in apprehension. The threatening posture he was describing has become known as a *deimatic* response (from the Greek word *deimos*, meaning fear) and many butterflies and moths that are cryptically coloured but conceal bright colours on their hind-wings show similar responses, accompanied by erratic body movements or changes in posture.

The Indian leaf butterfly, *Kallima inachus*, is a master magician that can make itself disappear, and re-appear just as suddenly. The upper side of the wings are bright with an iridescent blue sheen crossed by orange bands. The underside has an extraordinary resemblance to a leaf, including a stem, markings of leaf venation, and marks that look like decay and fungal attack. Alfred Russel Wallace described his frustration in trying to capture a specimen of this butterfly in his classic work *The Malay Archipelago* published in 1869:

> "…I often endeavoured to capture it without success, for after flying short distances it would enter a bush among dry or dead leaves, and however carefully I crept up to the spot I could never discover it till it would suddenly start out again and then disappear in a similar place. At length I was fortunate enough to see the exact spot where the butterfly settled, and though I lost sight of it for some time, I at length discovered that it was close before my eyes, but in that position of repose it so closely resembled a dead leaf attached to a twig as almost certainly to deceive the eye even when gazing full on it."

One factor that strongly influences the way in which colour is perceived is the nature of colour contrast, which is greatest between red and green, and yellow and blue. Organisms that need to be detected in order to ensure the survival of their species often contrast greatly with their environment. A ripe apple on the tree is easily detected, as is a yellow flower against the sky. Animals that are venomous or which sequester poisons are commonly red in colour. Red and

yellow appear bright against green vegetation because light from the sun is stronger in the green part of the spectrum after long wavelengths have been reduced by scattering, produced by water vapour in the air, and also because colours are perceived as more vivid when contrasted with colours further along the spectrum (red against green, for example). Hence reds and yellows are good colours for use in deimatic displays – like the yellow underwings that are displayed by a death's head hawk moth.

Charles Darwin confronted the problem of explaining the evolution of bright colour patterns in birds and insects, and decided that these must have evolved as a result of what he called sexual selection. He noted that in most of the very brightly coloured birds, including peacocks and pheasants, it was always the male that was the most beautifully attired. This view reflected the fact that during courtship of such species the female always has the prerogative of selecting her mate, and will select her companion purely on the basis of his looks, so it is always the most handsomely adorned male that gets to father offspring, and successive generations of females will weed out the dullards, and their genes with them. What continued to puzzle Darwin, however, were the many species in which both the males and the females displayed brilliant colours. To find the answer to this he had to turn to two of his contemporaries, Alfred Russel Wallace and Henry Walter Bates, who, along with him, were the three Titans of nineteenth-century zoology.

Wallace, who many (including myself) believe should be given as much credit as Darwin for originating the theory of evolution by natural selection, was a man of extraordinary achievements. While Darwin had the advantage of good means, connections and scientific patronage that enabled him to spend nearly five years travelling around South America on HMS *Beagle*, Wallace came from a relatively impoverished background, but saved enough money to travel to Brazil with his fellow entomologist Henry Walter Bates. Bates was only twenty-three at the time and Wallace twenty-two. The two men paid for their travels in the Amazon by assiduously collecting

The poisonous monarch butterfly (*Danaus plexippus*), a model copied by several other non-poisonous species

insects and birds, the majority of which were at that time unknown to science, and shipping them back to Britain, where most were bought by the Museum of Natural History. Wallace spent four years exploring the Amazon and Rio Negro, and Bates spent twelve years. Wallace's ship caught fire on his return journey to England. He was fortunate not to lose his life, but he did lose a trunk full of specimens and almost all his notebooks.

Undaunted, Wallace soon set off on his travels again, this time to explore the Malay Peninsula, which at that time included present-day Malaysia and Indonesia. He was the first to describe the 'wild man of Borneo', the orang-utan, and many new species of bird of paradise, but it was in Ternate in Indonesia that he wrote a letter to Darwin explaining his theory of evolution. The arrival of this letter threw Darwin into turmoil: he had been working on his draft of *Origin of Species* for many years, and realised he was about to be pipped at the post. The rest, as they say, is history. Despite the joint announcement of their theories, Darwin was able to get into print quickly, and because it was a thoroughly researched and painstaking work, published by John Murray, the pre-eminent scientific publisher of the Victorian era, Darwin's name prevailed as the most famous biologist of all time and Wallace's contemporaneous and parallel intellectual leap was eclipsed.

Wallace pointed out that many brightly-coloured insects also had stings or produced evil-smelling chemical secretions, and so in his view were advertising their distastefulness. While Wallace described many examples of mimicry among insects, including insects that were copies of totally unrelated species, which in a human context would be described as brilliant forgeries, it is Bates whose name became attached to the most striking form of visual mimicry in the animal kingdom. After Wallace had left the Amazon, Bates wrote a paper for the Linnaean Society in London on mimicry in butterflies. He sent a draft to Darwin, who wrote back to say "Your paper is too good for the ... common horde of entomologists." The paper marked the birth of the concept of Batesian mimicry, which continues to stimulate debate and research to the present day.

The basic concept of Batesian mimicry is that an insect that is highly poisonous forms the model for mimics that are not noxious, but which are the equivalent of wolves in sheep's clothing and therefore capitalise on the reputation of the model. The most familiar example of Batesian mimicry is the mimicking of wasps and hornets by harmless hover-flies, which almost invariably confuse the non-entomologist. Of these insects, the famous zoologist D'Arcy Thompson[v] wrote:

Much experimental work has been done to demonstrate how the poisons find their way into the model, how they are tolerated, and, most crucially, how insectivorous birds learn from what is literally bitter experience not to touch insects with particular colour patterns.

The classic research on this was done by Lincoln Brower and his colleagues, who made a special study of the monarch butterfly. This magnificent orange butterfly has excited tremendous interest because of its extraordinary migrations in North America. In the autumn, the butterflies on the East and West Coasts from as far north as Canada migrate southwards in millions and overwinter every year in the same locations to the south. The most famous site is the Valley of the Butterflies in Michoacán, not far from Mexico City. Their huge aggregations in pine trees, where they hibernate clinging to the Spanish moss, is one of the wonders of the natural world. In Taiwan the related blue crow butterflies (*Euploea*) undergo north-south migrations; each year part of a motorway is cordoned off during the spring northward migration to allow the insects to follow their age-old route without danger.

The monarch is highly poisonous: its tissues, particularly the wings, contain cardiac glycosides, toxins that paralyse the nervous system, affecting heart activity, as the name suggests. But the initial effect of the toxins is to make the unfortunate creature that has ingested them immediately violently ill and sick. The important point is that the predator does not die but survives with a life-long aversion to monarch butterflies. But an animal that has survived the poisons generalises the association with the insect it tried to eat, so that all large orange butterflies are likely to be avoided to a greater or lesser extent depending on their similarity to a monarch. Hence good mimics of the monarch are well protected once sufficient birds in a local population have experienced the pain of trying to eat a genuine monarch. The viceroy, an unrelated species once thought to be a Batesian mimic but now known to be poisonous, is easily confused with a monarch. In a survey of hundreds of photographs on the website Flickr by amateur photographers I found that over ten per cent of those labelled 'monarch' were actually viceroys: good testimony to the degree of resemblance of the two.

The monarch butterfly has a relative known as the queen butterfly (*Danaus gilippus*), which is also poisonous and looks very similar to the monarch. These two species are known as Müllerian mimics, after the naturalist Fritz Müller. Müller was a contemporary of Bates and Wallace who collected butterflies in Central America and Brazil, and noticed that there were many very similar species that were extremely abundant but apparently immune from predation. In 1878 he

above left: **The hornet clearwing moth (*Sesia apiformis*), a near-perfect mimic of the European hornet**

above right: **The Asian giant hornet, or 'Yak-killer' (*Vespa mandarinia*)**

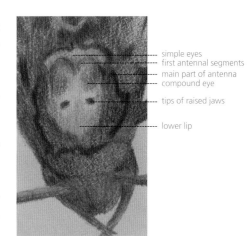

suggested that butterflies in these mimicry complexes were all distasteful to some extent, but benefited from adopting the same colours. Thus the negative experience of a bird with one species was likely to be associated with all similar species. The passion vine butterflies that Müller observed form large mimicry complexes. More will be said about these in Chapter 8.

The toxins that the monarchs contain are actually obtained from the food plants that the caterpillars feed on. The caterpillars have evolved immunity to these and sequester the toxins in their tissues, so that when the butterfly emerges from the chrysalis they are carried through and remain in the butterfly. More and more instances are being discovered of species of butterflies or moths feeding with immunity on poisonous plants and forming part of a Batesian mimicry complex.

The late Philip Shepherd, who made invaluable contributions to the understanding of mimicry in butterflies, once related that he had held a cocktail party in the West Indies in which the canapés were decorated with dead butterflies on cocktail sticks. Some were brightly coloured species, others drab browns. The non-biologists selected mostly the colourful morsels, while the biologists, who knew about warning colouration of poisonous insects, selected the dull-coloured ones. It seems that it is only as a result of instruction that we avoid bright colours. Berries and toadstools similarly stand out against the background and invite attention, but it is only as a result of warning from their parents that children avoid deadly nightshade and *Amanita* fungi; there is little evidence of instinctive aversion, and poisoning occurs regularly. This is unsurprising because most fruits and berries depend on being eaten for their survival, and children become quickly conditioned to associate red colours with food.

We see striped patterns more easily than patches of colour, and this may be true of animals as well. This is possibly because the black provides a high-contrast background, and because the colour signal is repeated, so it is a good signal for long-bodied animals such as snakes and wasps. The black and yellow stripes on the abdomen, with the same colours repeated on the hind-wings, above and below, suggest that the death's head hawk moth is a Batesian mimic of a wasp or a hornet.[vi] There are a number of such mimics in Europe, one of the most striking being the hornet clearwing moth, which bears a near-perfect resemblance to the common hornet. However, there are difficulties when it comes to the hawk moth. First, it is much larger than the European hornet, and second, all species of hornet in Western Europe and Africa, where the moth is most common, have black or dark brown heads, and the moth has no black head marking to fit onto the hornet-like body.

In 1972, Walter Linsenmaier published a beautifully illustrated book called *Insects of the World*. I have often browsed through my copy at the end of a long day and found relaxation and inspiration in the superb watercolour reproductions. After pondering on the issue of hornets for some time

clockwise from top left:

The head of the Asian giant hornet (*Vespa mandarinia*)

Close-up of the skull marking of the death's head hawk moth

Diagram to show the features of the hornet's head replicated in the moth

I had a sudden recollection that Linsenmaier had figured a white-headed hornet. Indeed he had; one of the New World species was called the bald-faced hornet and had a white head. But on the next page was just what I was looking for: the Japanese giant hornet, the largest and most ferocious hornet in the world with a yellowish-white head and black eyes! This insect has a powerful and painful sting. Multiple stings can be lethal, and approximately seventy Japanese die from them every year.

To understand what the death's head hawk moth is to another animal, we have to first reject the interpretation that your and my brain has made automatically – that it is a moth – and focus on the detail without the preconception, following my hypothesis that a predator starts with the detail and constructs the final image like a child with a simple jigsaw. The background colour of the thorax is black, so that the skull mark stands out in high contrast and is the most vivid symbol. With the wings closed, there are other white markings, particularly the presumptive cross-bones.

Close inspection of the hornet shows many features that correspond with those of the moth, the most striking being the black compound eyes that are similar to the 'eye-sockets' of the 'skull'. But it was not until I got to the final draft of this book that I suddenly realised that I had made a wrong assumption in this perception. Although the skull and cross-bones marking does resemble a skull in many respects when the moth is viewed with the head up, the resemblance is more striking when viewed in the head-down position. The sketch shows the features of the hornet reproduced in the skull. The two small black 'eyes' now become the black tips of the jaws, which are opened and thrust forward in defence or attack, and the cheeks of the skull copy the black, slightly reflective compound eyes. The 'cross-bones' are now obvious representations of the long second segment of the antennae (the *scape*) which is yellow-orange in the hornet; the remaining segments are usually bent downwards and are less visible because they are black. The black segments form what is known as the *funiculus*, and they cannot be moved one upon the other, but they can be moved on the scape, and the articulation between the scape and the funiculus is clearly discernable on the moth.

As we shall see later, the human visual system prefigures images so we tend to make the assumption that the 'skull' on the moth is in the same head-up position as the moth itself. A lizard, for example, confronting the moth head-on, will see the hornet's head from exactly the same perspective as it would see a real hornet.

I shall digress at this point to explain why the giant hornet is such a fearsome creature. It is the *Tyrannosaurus* of the insect world, but unlike that dinosaur it hunts in dense packs. It preys upon other wasps, hornets, and bees, which are themselves important insect predators. Japanese bee-keepers have a major problem each year preventing their colonies from being annihilated by the hornets. The hornets have scouts, which search for bee hives. When one is found, the scout marks it with a pheromone from a gland on the underside of the abdomen. The pheromone is simply a scent mark that is recognised by other hornets in the colony, and this attracts other hornets, which group together before making a mass attack on the hive. They kill the bees one by one by stinging them and tearing them apart with their jaws. The dead bees are then ferried back to the hornets' nest, where they are chewed up and given as food to the grub-like larvae.

After successful initial attacks, more pheromone is added, stepping up the recruitment of hornets, and in this way a colony of thirty thousand honeybees can be massacred by only thirty hornets.

The giant hornet is so admired for its dominance and power that a Japanese company has marketed a product called 'Vaam' containing the essential amino acids in a peculiar secretion that the larvae produce as a food supplement for the adult workers. It is claimed that the amino acids facilitate the metabolism of fat in the human body to form energy-rich compounds that are needed when energy reserves run low. Some Japanese Olympic athletes have taken Vaam and believe it has helped them to generate energy quickly and improve their performance.

For every powerful poison or weapon of tooth or claw, it seems that nature provides a protection for some. The ubiquitous European honeybee has no defence against this marauder, but the related Asiatic honeybee, *Apis cerana*, a species that nests in hollow trees and has evolved alongside the giant hornet, has an amazing defence strategy. It is able to detect the hornet marker pheromone, so that when it is produced bee workers converge on the site and take on the hornets one by one, so that a ball of up to five hundred bees may form around a single hornet. In the middle of that ball the temperature gradually rises as a result of the activity of the bees and soon reaches 47°C, which is several degrees higher than the boiling point of the body fluids of the hornet. So it dies. The bees can withstand a temperature a few degrees higher than the hornets and they survive.

What makes the death's head hawk moth such a fascinating creature is that by moving slightly its wings and body it can suggest that it is something different. Look again closely at the lines forming the 'collar bones' below the skull marking and they are seen to become the shoulder of a limb continuing out laterally as white 'legs' on the forewings. They are matched by a pair of apparent white hind legs pictured near the wing tips. The fore-wings delineate a lighter cone-shaped zone where the hind-wings are exposed, and now you see the image of a lizard-like vertebrate.

When it opens its wings slightly, the bright yellow and black tiger stripes on the abdomen come into view; another jigsaw piece that turns it suddenly into a Japanese hornet rather than a lizard and the slim wing folds alongside the abdomen suggest the folded dusky wings of the hornet. If the moth is alarmed, it flaps its wings, turning towards one side and the other, multiplying the intensity of the hornet signal.

Those practised in solving the puzzles in children's books such as 'How many faces can you see in this picture?' will find it rewarding to examine the death's head hawk moth more closely. The 'skull and crossbones' viewed in the head-up position of the moth provide the image of another venomous animal: a giant centipede perhaps, with two small black eyes with what look like black opened jaws with sharp tips, like the poison claws of *Scolopendra* centipedes. Many tropical centipedes are in fact banded in black and yellow like the abdomen of the moth.

The moth has at least three more impersonations, and there may be others that I have missed. It will close its wings so it appears as black as possible, and run around in a zigzag pattern squeaking like a mouse; and it can rear up its front end waving its hairy black front legs in the air like a large spider. The latter impression is heightened by the white bands on the forelegs, which are reminiscent of those on the legs of some of the large poisonous mygalomorph spiders, including tarantulas. Apart from the colouring, which is similar to that of a bat, brown lines on the wings trace out the bone pattern in the wings of a bat.

Now the obvious point here is that you see these apparitions only if you throw away the assumption that your mind has made for you, after analysing all the sensory input to the optic lobes in your brain and cross-matching it with all the pre-formed schemata or models or whatever you want to call them in the brain, and putting into your consciousness that this is some sort of moth. This is an instantaneous process unless there is an ambiguity in the image and then the ambiguity or illusion takes time for you to resolve.

For us, the ambiguity in the moth is at a very low level, because you already 'know' that it is a moth, so scrutiny to determine what kind of moth and what the markings are is a secondary process. Not so for a predatory animal. The ambiguity is high for the animal because it is confronting image fragments, which can change from one moment to the next and do not build up easily to a coherent whole. It follows very simply from this that the moth may frighten us because we have a strong emotional response to the skull as a symbol of death, while to a bird the skull by itself is not frightening at all, but it is there because it is the centrepiece of a masquerade that may sabotage the perceptual process much as surrealist art does in our visual world. The death's head hawk moth, though, is not the only such masquerade among butterflies and moths. Evolution has fashioned many such fascinating masquerades and tangled webs of deceit from the wings of these insects which have hitherto been overlooked.

The Devil
in
the Detail

"The eye, like the groping hand, scans the page, and the cues or messages it elicits are used by the questioning mind to narrow down uncertainties. Every piece of information that reaches us through the senses can thus be used to answer a further question and remove a further doubt."

E H Gombrich: *Meditations on a Hobby Horse*

"When an animal or an autistic person is seeing the real world instead of his idea of the world that means he's seeing detail. This is the single most important thing to know about the way animals perceive the world: animals see details people don't see. They are totally detail-orientated. That's the key."

Temple Grandin: *Animals in Translation*

A t this point I have to confess to a certain attraction to anthropomorphism – viewing animal behaviour from a human perspective. This is generally considered a cardinal sin among scientists, and for very good reasons. Prior to the twentieth century the study of animal behaviour was anecdotal, and with that went the assumption that animals were possessed, to a greater or lesser degree, of intelligence and planned their actions as any human being would. The Church baulked at this because of the implications that animals had souls and were therefore with us in the queue for salvation. Strong refutation came from the philosopher René Descartes in his *Discourse on Method*:

> *"...after the error of those who deny the existence of God ... there is none that is more powerful in leading feeble minds astray from the straight path of virtue than the supposition that the soul of brutes is of the same nature as our own; and consequently that after this life we have nothing to hope for or fear, more than flies and ants."*

In the early twentieth century, people put the lid on it all by insisting, rightly, that there were much simpler explanations for seemingly intelligent behaviour in animals. A famous example that has frequently found its way into textbooks of animal behaviour was that of a horse called 'Clever Hans' that was capable of doing simple arithmetic and answering questions about such things as calendar dates, spelling of words and musical notes by tapping its foot. The questions were given either verbally (in German) or written on paper. When psychologists investigated, they found that the horse could not solve these problems if it could not see its owner, or if the owner did not himself know the answer. Unknown to him, the horse was picking up unconscious signals from his face and posture that appeared after the horse had tapped the appropriate number of times.

The view developed that animals lower on the evolutionary scale were driven solely by instincts – blueprints for action that are inherited and reside in the animal brain – and it was proposed that to some extent similar instincts reside in the human brain. The role of instinct in the behaviour of insects was demonstrated vividly by the French entomologist and writer Jean-Henri Fabre. Fabre was a brilliant naturalist who retired from schoolteaching to a villa in Carpentras near Avignon in southern France, and was to spend the rest of his life observing and writing about insects in his garden and in the fields around. As we saw in Chapter 4, he had the poet's gift of

previous page: **The great peacock moth (*Saturnia pyri*). The large eye-spots on a background the colour of owl feathers are superimposed on the pale image of a bird with a spread tail, about to land**

above: **An Atala butterfly (*Eumaeus atala*) with bright spots that appear almost luminescent**

opposite: **Underside of the wings of the poisonous gulf fritillary (*Agraulis vanillae*) showing reflective markings that may mimic vertebrate teeth**

explaining things evocatively and wrote biographies of the crickets, praying mantids, bees, wasps, beetles and other creatures that he came across, chronicling their daily lives and their social interactions. He gave one of the first detailed accounts of pheromones, in this case the sexual attractant scent produced by the female of the great peacock moth, which he found could attract males from a kilometre or more away. As a result of many hours of patient observation and simple experiments he was able to show that insects tend to react to simple stimuli they encounter by engaging in a stereotyped sequence of actions typical of the species. This laid the basis for the development of ethology: the scientific study of animal behaviour. This was the science of which, as we have seen, Lorenz and Tinbergen were the recognised founders and which had its origins in observation of animals in their own domain.

Ethology was essentially a riposte to the development of 'behaviourism' by comparative psychologists during the earlier part of the twentieth century. Psychologists such as J.B. Watson took the view that man was born with a brain for which there was no inherited script, but simply an enormous capacity to acquire behavioural responses through interaction with his environment. This was satirised in Aldous Huxley's *Brave New World*, in which Huxley envisioned incubators with infants undergoing artificially controlled formation into social categories of 'alphas, betas and gammas'. Then the pendulum swung back some way again, receiving its impetus from the writings of Konrad Lorenz and Niko Tinbergen who promulgated the opposing view that behaviour could develop either from genetic information (instinct) or from information acquired from the environment (learning), with a large preponderance of learnt components in man and the higher apes. The simple empirical approach that naturalists such as Fabre had developed, and which had a strong anthropomorphic flavour to it, was thereafter dominated by theoretical models of behaviour, which inevitably became less and less useful as many ethologists lost their links to nature. Throughout the latter half of the twentieth century biologists argued over whether behaviour was really either instinctive or learnt, until the ethologist Patrick Bateson trenchantly pointed out that it was as useless arguing about whether a certain type of behaviour was one or the other as it was trying to decide which bits of a cake were flour or eggs.

Given the way in which science jumps from one framework of dogma to another, it is sadly true that you will search almost endlessly for references to Jean-Henri Fabre's books in scientific journals or textbooks of animal behaviour, and only a very few will turn up.

Trying to put yourself into the mind of an animal is still scientific heresy, but ironically, ethology originated from the Greek word *ethologia*, which was applied to the study of human character, but modern ethology deferred to psychologists when it came to human behaviour. Hence the schism between man and animals has been perpetuated in the last fifty years. It was accepted that you could learn about the well-springs of human behaviour by studying animals, but not the converse. But we know now that the genetic make-up of primates is almost identical to that of humans, humans sharing 98.4 per cent of their genome with chimpanzees, so Descartes' view of animals as kinds of machine that, unlike humans, work out their lives like the actions of a wound-up clock, has few followers today.

Until relatively recently, philosophers and psychologists postulated that only human beings had a concept of self, by which they usually meant something like a sense of individual existence, separate, in the example of a very young child, from the mother. As far as animals are concerned, we see the essence of this process in signs of recognition of their own image in a mirror, when they respond to it differently from the way they respond to another of the same species. Your dog or cat will not respond to its own image in a mirror, although it may be momentarily arrested by the apparent movement of the reflected image. Primates, dolphins and elephants though, alone in the animal kingdom, share with us a sense of self, and can recognise their own images in a mirror. The higher primates, chimpanzees, bonobos and gorillas especially, when reared from infancy by humans, can be trained to hold a conversation with simple syntax and to express their feelings to humans by using a keyboard. That schism between man and animals that Darwin first sought to close is becoming smaller and smaller. Comparative psychology is becoming less of a one-way street, and anthropocentricity, the development of a more empathetic type of relationship with animals, is leading to new understandings.

We humans commonly have fears, or phobias, of snakes, spiders and other venomous animals, and our imaginations are dominated by the fear that monsters such as dragons, chimaeras, dinosaurs and lions inspire within us. The devil himself – the apotheosis of terror – has been portrayed often with the body of a goat, cloven hooves, bats' wings, and claws. In view of the evidence of mind in some animals, we are entitled to ask whether these fears were generated in us in the same ways as they are generated in animals, or whether they are archetypal images which are in some way preformed in everyone's imagination.

The American animal behaviourist Temple Grandin has published a book which attempts to answer this question.[i] What is really refreshing about her book is that it cuts across the dogma of mainstream ethological thinking. Temple Grandin's explanations for the peculiarities of animal behaviour will take a long time to find acceptance by biologists because they are very largely founded on subjective interpretation and hypothesis, rather than the results of empirical research and replicated experiments; but then so was *On the Origin of Species*.

Temple Grandin achieved fame in the world of animal behaviour, becoming a University Professor and Consultant to some of the world's largest companies involved in animal husbandry. She is autistic, and in her studies came to the realisation that she, and many people like her, perceive the world in a similar way to animals. She explains that while a normal person will see what she terms a *schema* – the whole picture if you like, an autistic person is often unable to see that, but sees the details in disassembled form first. Perception is thus a relatively slow process and can actually be overwhelmingly complex to the person concerned. Referring to a description by Donna Williams, an autistic person who is the author of *Nobody Nowhere*,[ii] Grandin explains,

> "She sees a kind of slide show of the object. If she's looking at a tree, first she might see the branch on that tree, then the scene changes and she sees a bird sitting on the branch, then the scene changes again and she sees some leaves, and so on."

In her book *Autism and Sensing* Donna herself elaborates on this, explaining that until the age of four she saw only fragments and not their context:

above left: **The Gulf fritillary butterfly (*Agraulis vanillae*) has reflective spots like tiny mirrors in stark contrast to the repetitive black spots on an orange background**

above right: **Chrysalis of the common crow butterfly (*Euploea core*) with a mirror-like surface**

"I'd see the nostril but lose the concept of nose, see the nose but lose the face, see the fingernail but lose the finger."[iii]

In later life she found talking to a large audience highly intimidating because of the maelstrom of individual images before her that she could not assimilate and see as an audience. Only through unifying the images by visualising them as parts of a kind of tree was she able to cope.

Vision in humans, from our own experience, is much more of an interpretative or imaginative process than in animals. Indeed, the word 'imagination' derives from the Latin word *imago*,[iv] which is a copy or representation, in this case made by the mind. Our ability to see what Grandin calls the 'whole picture' of something corresponds with what psychologists call *Gestalt* perception. *Gestalt* is a German word meaning 'form or figure', and the meaning here is that the whole we perceive is more than the sum of the parts, or, in other words, it has imagination built into it, and therefore it is quite difficult for most of us to pick out detail in what we normally are used to seeing in a work of art, or a map for instance. During the Second World War, autistic people were found to be more adept than normal people at detecting fine details in aerial photographs.

One consequence of the impact of detail on vertebrate perception, Grandin points out, is that animals are disturbed to the point of panic by bright objects that are in unexpected places. For example, a piece of glass reflecting sunlight in the path of cattle was sufficient to repel the animals and cause complete turmoil. She was able to perceive the cause of their panic only by following their path on her hands and knees. Such a reaction may well explain the highly reflective spots on the wings of the so-called metal-mark and fritillary butterflies, and reflective spots on the chrysalis of some butterflies. The crow butterflies of South-East Asia have a chrysalis that

reflects light like a silvered mirror. We can only speculate on whether reflected light mirrors the pattern of the surrounding vegetation in which the chrysalis is suspended, or whether the intensity of the reflection is a disturbing feature.

In contrast to many people with autism, the brain of a normal person will process the myriad items of sensory information it receives every moment, and synthesise an image of which that person is conscious. He or she will immediately see a tree because the brain adds up all the features that go to make up what you have learned a tree is generally composed of, and unlocks, as Aldous Huxley might have put it, the door to perception of trees. It is like, on the one hand, seeing the separated pieces of a jigsaw puzzle and attempting to make sense of them, and on the other hand, of having the brain mechanisms to put them all together for you. In doing the latter, the brain will sometimes make a mistake or fill in the missing pieces itself and build the 'wrong' picture, as happens when we are deceived by illusions.

Grandin emphasises that the brain sees what it expects to see. We can see no more vivid illustration of this phenomenon than in the distressing affliction of *anorexia nervosa*, the eating disorder that affects mainly young women. This involves obsession with body image. The person concerned develops a strong conviction that she is unattractive and overweight. Seeing herself in a mirror paradoxically reinforces that conviction even though she may be emaciated to the point of her own survival being threatened. The brain in this case rejects the image that the eyes present and presents instead a distorted bogus image that the mind accepts as reality. Sometimes, tragically, this bogus image cannot be corrected by therapy and the person risks death by starvation.

The influence of the human brain's preconceptions is so great that when we see something that has the right parameters of size, shape and movement to suggest a butterfly, we then expect to see a butterfly, and it is difficult to override that expectation. The swallowtail on page 96 is

immediately a butterfly to us, but examine it from a different angle, as on page 97, as a bird might do without any preconception. First you see a pair of eyes, then a pointed snout, then whiskers at the tip of the snout. Your brain's first hypothesis may be that this is a rodent. We humans (with the possible exception of those with autism) find this interpretation very hard to accept because we use the details to refine the general picture that we have already subscribed to, while a bird will use the details to construct the general picture.

This phenomenon of preconception is at the root of numerous visual illusions, including the well-known vase-face illusion. It requires concentrated mental effort to switch from one interpretation to the other.

A related phenomenon known as 'inattentional blindness' was illustrated by the famous 'gorillas in our midst' experiment[v] in which subjects were shown a video of a basketball game and asked to count the number of passes. Some way into the video a woman in a gorilla suit walked up in front of the camera beating her breast. Fifty per cent of the viewers were unaware of the gorilla, which didn't fit into the picture the brain had constructed and was busy with: that is, they had not seen it. Or perhaps we should say they were not aware of having seen it. Subliminal advertising follows similar principles, and it has been shown that an image can be committed to memory providing that the brain is not already preoccupied with other things. In other words, it sometimes works but we are never conscious of it.

These intriguing new insights from psychological disciplines fit in well with what we know about visual perception in animals from experimental studies in mainstream ethology, which, as we have seen, show that animals react to very simple stimuli (sign stimuli). The fact is that animals do not need to see the whole picture, just key identifiers. For example, I mentioned earlier that colour alone is sufficient to provoke aggressive behaviour in some territorial male birds. A well-known example is to be found in robins, and I was once buzzed by a male hummingbird that seemed to take exception to my bright green camera bag. There are records of male pheasants and grouse chasing red cars. Cocker and Mabey in *Birds Britannica* refer to a grouse which attacked red hiking boots, red coats and red rucksacks, a vivid illustration of the fact that the male bird has no preformed mental image of another male.

When a bird looks at a moth, we can surmise that it sees the details first – the eye-spots, the waspish stripes, or whatever happens to be there. Those details determine whether the moth is treated as food or danger, not whether it fits into the human schema of a moth. The difference is that you and I know that the death's head is a moth because we have the mental image of a generalised moth, just as we know that a red sock is not a male grouse.

Now it follows from the findings of the ethologists, as they are confirmed by Grandin, that the simple sign stimulus to which animals are most likely to respond vigorously – eye-spots, reptile head markings, bird beaks, etc., do not need to be arranged in the frame of the insect's wings in a co-ordinated whole to be effective. Each feature will be seen, at least initially, in isolation from the rest: the whole is only the sum of the parts for an animal, not more than that. Hence there can be many eye-spots on an insect, or there can be, as in the death's head hawk moth and others, a combination of wasp and reptilian or other predator features, examples of which we shall see in the following chapter. Small insectivorous birds have small eyes with a short focal length and are therefore short-sighted. At close distance even a small eye-spot must appear large in their visual field.

In this way of seeing things, size is apparently not relevant because animals (and to some extent autistic people), according to Grandin, are hyperspecific and over-generalise. What 'hyperspecific' means is that their classification of objects is very narrow, so that while, for example, normal people recognise all breeds of dogs as dogs, an autistic person would have a much narrower concept and treat a dachshund as something different from a dog. What 'over-generalisation' (a concept of LeDoux, see below) means is that generalisation – making connections between similar objects or any kind of stimulus and putting them into the same category – goes too far. We over-generalise when we see every striped insect as a wasp, or every young person in jeans as a student. Animals, says Grandin, over-generalise but are hyperspecific in doing so. A dog she knew was once badly frightened by a hot air balloon that revved up its burners above her. That dog over-generalised thereafter to anything round and red against a

blue sky, even if it was only a tiny speck in the sky. It does not generalise to other objects that float around in the sky such as blue balloons, red birds or aeroplanes, just to round red things, which provoke intense fear regardless of their other resemblances to hot air balloons. This leads us to the conclusion that, for example, a predator will generalise to 'wasp' stripes, but will not generalise between a wasp and a stripe-free insect the same size and shape.

How often in your life have you said, "At first sight I thought it was (a puma, aeroplane, bird, someone I know, etc....)". This is an admission that your initial interpretations needed verifying. This, according to Grandin, is another key to the understanding of the behaviour of animals, one in this instance that is forged from the neurological research of Joseph LeDoux.[vi] He found evidence that there are two separate nervous pathways from sense organs to the part of the brain (the amygdala) that controls fear responses. The fast pathway goes from the sense organs to the thalamus, which passes the information immediately to the amygdala, the whole process taking twelve milliseconds. So you could react immediately to what appears to be a snake in front of you without thinking. The slow pathway diverts the information through the cerebral hemispheres, which then analyse it and in effect confirm or deny whether it is really a snake or, for example, a harmless length of rope. This process takes twice as long, and so would considerably increase your chances of getting bitten by a snake if you had only that perceptual mechanism to rely on. The fast automatic response is clearly more important for survival and does not demand a highly developed cerebral cortex. Hence, it is likely to be what most animals rely upon for self-protection, and that helps us to understand why mimicry of venomous animals can be so effective. Equally importantly, it helps to explain why that mimicry can be effective even though it is imperfect.

As a consequence of the need to identify danger or a possible predator quickly, many animals, like us, appear to have developed the ability to identify an image when they can see just part of it. The image opposite illustrates this. At least to someone who has studied natural history, it is immediately clear that there is the head of a large stag beetle: you do not need to see the rest of the beast, but to confirm the point it is on the next page. This reinforces the suggestion that just part of an animal pictured on a butterfly's wing will invite an interpretation of the whole, especially in dim light or if the butterfly is partially concealed.

We must be wary, however, in stretching anthropomorphism to the point at which we assume that animals make the kind of extrapolations that we do. A stag beetle calls forth associated images of stags, and masculinity, which it cannot do in animals. The representation of something by presenting only part of it, which works because we easily call to mind the rest of the object, is known as *metonymy*. Metonymy plays a greater part in our lives than most people realise, expressions like 'the crown', 'the White House', 'the Cross' and so forth, being parts used to represent something greater.[vii] Turner[viii] found that parrots are of great importance in the social and spiritual life of the Bororo Amazonian tribe because they signify the soul and flight. Red macaw feathers are highly prized and collected and worn as a representation of the parrot and the spiritual world that it stands for. Thus we alone, as human beings, can build up tiers of meanings from seeing part of something: the extrapolation can go far beyond completing the picture.

Humans alone have the ability, which we know as 'art', to make representations of objects and scenes outside the mind, which although they may not be true likenesses may serve to trigger images already in the mind and the experiences, feelings and emotions connected with them. We produce icons, such as religious icons, maps, photographs, road signs warning of ducks, cows, or old people in the road, that resemble the object, which, although they may be simplified or stylised, conjure up associations and remembrances of things past.

The 'imagination' of the mind at work in metonymy is a device frequently used in art, where the illustration of a hand or part of a face is sufficient to make us see the whole person. Indeed, a figure that has been painted so as to appear in the distance, with no facial features, we see as complete, the mind filling in the eyes, nose and so forth. This extrapolation is made easier if there is an area without any figures in it on which the mind can paint the rest of the picture. An example of this is in the paintings of the fifteenth-century Flemish artist, Petrus Christus, as in his *Portrait of a Young Man* in which glimpses of the landscape are seen through parts of windows and *Virgin and Child in a Domestic Interior* in which parts of bedrooms and gardens are seen, and

An object largely hidden by the tree can be interpreted easily

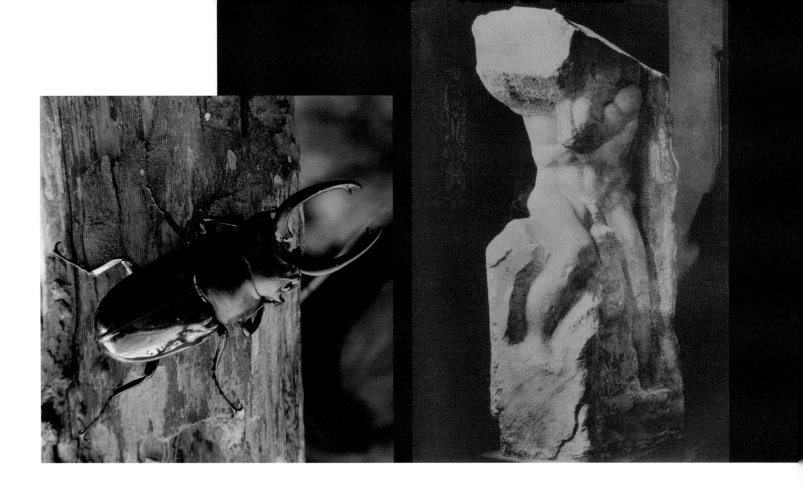

your mind supplies the rest of the image. A painting by Max Ernst, A*u premier mot limpide*, originally used in a room decoration, has a hand coming through a window. We know immediately that this is a woman's hand, and the sexual imagery in the painting guides the construction of the image of the woman, calling on previous experiences and stored images.

The Guardian newspaper in 2008 published a photograph of the American Vice-President, Dick Cheney, on a fishing trip, which showed a reflection in his sun-glasses of what some people thought were naked women. When this image was displayed on an Internet website, nearly 60 per cent of respondents voted for the interpretation of 'hot babe sunbathing'. Expert photographic analysis, however, revealed that the reflection was of Cheney's hand on a fishing rod and the more exciting conclusion was therefore constructed in the mind of the observers on the basis of very limited information. A similar reconstructive process comes into play in interpreting words. The majority of people may be able to read this: you olny rqueire the fsrit and lsat lttseres of a wrod to konw waht it is bceusae the bairn aealdry has an igmae to mtach it asingat. The first and last letters of a word are enough to trigger an image that the brain already holds.

Michelangelo created unique three-dimensional illusory human forms in his sculptures *The Prisoners*, some of which are in the Accademia Gallery in Florence. These statues were created as part of the monumental tomb of Pope Julius II, but in the end were not incorporated in it. They were sculpted from huge blocks of marble in such a way that they are partly formed and appear to be crystallising out of the stone. The analogy with butterflies emerging from the chrysalis, their wings just beginning to unfold is striking, especially as the sculptures are said to represent the liberation of the soul from the material world. Again, in sculpture the perception of the human form that appears to have only just been begun by the artist depends on the brain completing it.

When the pictorial or other representation of something has been changed so much from the original that we need extra information to interpret it, then it becomes known as a symbol. What is normally understood by a symbol is an object that through conventional and repeated use comes to represent or stand for something different. Many of the symbols that are important to us today in western society are material objects that have become indicators of wealth or success: the Managing Director's Jaguar, his wife's Astra, and his son's Cobra sports car are all part

left: **The funerary mask of Tutankhamun, incorporating the king cobra, an emblem of Lower Egypt**

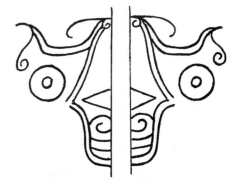

of their 'image'. Away and beyond the materialistic societies in which many of us live today, other jaguars, stars and snakes are also symbols, but with different meanings and associations. The symbols of power were animals that were feared and admired, so much so that they became gods and goddesses in pantheistic religions, surviving today in the Hindu religion, as, for example, Hanuman the monkey god, Naga the snake god, and Ganesh the elephant-headed god (who is part elephant, part mouse, and part snake). The ancient Egyptians conceived the falcon-headed god, Horus, the jackal-headed god, Anubis, the cat-headed god, Bastet, and many others. The images of these gods incorporated a variety of animals, including the king cobra, scorpion, lion, leopard, sacred ibis, and scarab beetle.

The oldest evidence for the use of symbols goes back two million years to *homo habilis* from the Olduvai gorge. Mary Leakey found a small stone that showed evidence of having been worked by hand, and appeared to represent the head of a baboon. Baboons were no doubt a threat to early man, and J.B. Harrod[ix] advanced the theory that, because the head was pitted with holes, it was used for magical purposes, making an analogy with the witchcraft practised in some African tribes who stuck needles into the image of a person or animal to bring about their death. Harrod has also argued that the geometry of chipped stone tools of early humans indicates an aesthetic sense, and also a means of communication of feelings by the shapes of the cut edges, which are often more elaborate than is necessary for their use as tools, but symbolise gestures and facial expressions, becoming the forerunners of hieroglyphs. The analogue that has been incorporated into more modern art is the use of scalloped upward curving lines to signify optimism, or a smile, and of downwardly curving lines to signify the converse. Chinese pictures and symbols have been found among the 8,400 cliff paintings in Damaidi, northern China, that incorporate hieroglyphs between ten and sixteen thousand years old and provide key elements of modern Chinese. Those that have been deciphered represent the sun, moon and stars, spiritual characters, and hunting, dancing and sacrifice. In modern Chinese the sun is represented by a circle with a spot in the middle, so it also suggests an eye, as it does in Egyptian hieroglyphs where it is a circle within a circle. It has also been argued[x] that the first elements of Chinese pictographs were developed to annotate the life cycle and mass rearing procedures of sericulture. In bronze vessels of the sixth century BC, which held hot water to soften the cocoon silk, there are designs of a moth with two large eye-spots. This is intriguing because the domestic silk moth and the related species *Bombyx mandarina*, from which it is almost certainly descended, have no eye spots on the wings. This may refer to species of A*ntheraea*, which are used to produce Tasar silk.

If we look at the patterns found on the wings of butterflies and moths we find that some are obviously iconic: eye-spots, for example. Others we find only if we isolate the detail, when we see features of birds, snakes, lizards, monkeys, scorpions, etc. These are like Michelangelo's *Prisoners*, part-figures that the brain can complete; there can be little doubt that many animals can do the same.

But for us these figures are not just representations of the animals concerned, they are also archetypal symbols that mean immeasurably more to us humans than snake, owl or scorpion, and are the cornerstones of our religions and cultures.

above: **Design from a Chinese bronze container used for separating silk, in which eye-spots, antennae and the body of an insect are figured**

opposite: **The Chinese oak silk moth (*Antheraea mylitta*) with eyed wings, a source of Tasar silk**

Confusing Messages

"'Well! I've often seen a cat without a grin,' thought Alice; 'but a grin without a cat! It's the most curious thing I ever saw in all my life!'"

Lewis Carroll: *Alice's Adventures in Wonderland*

"Among these things, one thing seems certain — that nothing certain exists and there is nothing more pitiful or more presumptuous than man."

Pliny the Elder

earlier introduced the hypothesis that the moth is a Batesian mimic of the giant hornet, but if that is accepted it leaves us with some important new questions. Why is the resemblance of the hornet image quite a poor one to our eyes, and why, if we can see immediately that it is a moth, can a predator not see the same?

The answer to the first question comes in a paper[i] I wrote some years ago on a concept my colleague John Allen and I called 'Satyric mimicry'. This was an attempt to explain the findings of some experimental work by Dittrich and his colleagues at Exeter University[ii] on hover flies. Some hover fly species are near-perfect visual mimics of wasps, but some show only a slight resemblance, looking more like houseflies, and there are many intermediates. The unexpected finding had been that the 'intermediates' were apparently as well protected as the near-perfect mimics. It was clear to me that the pattern of results fitted the interpretation that the intermediates were ambiguous, neither obviously fly nor obviously wasp.

For us, such images create troubling illusions. One good example that perhaps helps to explain the action of satyric mimicry comes from the psychologist Gerald Fisher who produced a series of images at one end showing a man's head and the other a kneeling woman. Mid-way in the series the figures have maximum ambiguity and are perceived as either the head or the woman, the mind oscillating between the two and unable to resolve the image.

From the 1970s onwards, the tobacco companies, in particular, produced a type of advertisement – found on every billboard and in every popular magazine – that attracted attention because of its surrealistic nature. The advertisers copied the techniques of the surrealists to puzzle and shock our perception. They succeeded in separating the message and the product. The main image was simply a curiosity-arousing vehicle, which led the eye to the product in one corner. The technique that was used was to present a familiar object in an unfamiliar context, or to juxtapose two objects that are normally never seen together. This causes a breakdown in the process of perception, making the interpretation of the meaning very puzzling, and holding our attention for much longer than normal.

Gallaghers were among the pioneers of surrealist advertising for their Silk Cut cigarette brand. Paul Arden, who worked for the advertising company Saatchi and Saatchi introduced the image of cut purple silk, the brand's signature being purple.[iii] This was used in still-life photographs with no script except for the Government health warning.

previous page: **The narrow-bordered bee hawk moth (*Hemaris tityus*), mimic of a large bumble-bee**

above: **Fisher's illusion. The perceived image changes near the middle of the series. The exact point of change may differ according to whether you scan from left to right, or vice versa, but the closer you are to that point the more time you need to reach a decision**

The common image is of silk with a cut in it, so it is a rebus-type puzzle, the solution giving the name of the brand. But at the same time there is an affront to the perception produced by the need to reconcile the mind's image of cigarettes with a damaged piece of silk. David Lodge in his satirical novel *Nice Work* has an amusing discussion between his two characters on the semiotics of this type of advertisement, which begins with the statement that the silk, with its voluptuous curves and sensuous texture symbolises the human body, and the elliptical slit is obviously a vagina.

> Vic says: *'You must have a twisted mind to see that in a perfectly harmless bit of cloth.'*
> Robyn replies: *'What's the point of it then?.... Why use cloth to advertise cigarettes?'*
> [Vic] *'Well, that's the name of 'em, isn't it? Silk Cut. It's a picture of the name. Nothing more or less.'*
> *'Suppose they'd used a picture of a roll of silk cut in half – would that do just as well?'*
> *'I suppose so. Yes, why not?'*
> *'Because it would look like a penis cut in half, that's why'*

The conversation switches to the search for hidden meanings, and continues:

> *'… A cigarette is a cigarette. A piece of silk is a piece of silk. Why not leave it at that?'*
> *'When they're represented they acquire additional meanings… Signs are never innocent. Semiotics teaches us that.'*
> *'Semi-what?'*
> *'Semiotics. The study of signs.'*
> *'It teaches us to have dirty minds. If you ask me.'*

clockwise from top left: **A queen wasp (*Paravespula germanica*): a model for many species of hoverfly**

Volucella inanis, a hoverfly which is a close wasp and hornet mimic

Temnostoma bombylans – a poor wasp mimic

Episyrphus balteatus, another hoverfly that has been considered an imperfect mimic of a wasp

Syrphus ribesii, a hoverfly in which the wasp markings are less pronounced; it is not obviously a wasp or a fly on casual inspection

After a time, like David Lodge's characters, I too became bored with this game when I was driving to work each morning, at least until the advertisement changed. Gradually, this advertising technique was taken up by other companies, including Marlborough and the American brewery Michelob. Advertisements of the latter included bottles of their beer dressed up to look like skittles, cotton bobbins and so forth, thus presenting ambiguous images that were entertaining and intriguing.

One of the most famous advertisements of Benson and Hedges was of a gold cigarette packet outside a mouse hole (supplanting the image of a mouse-trap). Others included a packet of cigarettes in a birdcage (with a bird's shadow cast on the wall behind it), and a golden sunset over Egyptian pyramids in which one pyramid is a gold packet of cigarettes set at an appropriate angle.

Whatever other messages the surrealist advertisements may have had – either related to sexual desires, or fear of death, or to the luxury of silk and gold – they succeeded in generating puzzlement and intrigue either through the positioning of a familiar object (usually the product) in an unusual context, or by presenting ambiguous images. When such advertisements became part of the urban landscape in the 1990s, I gradually realised that I was experiencing a reaction to them somewhat similar to that which a bird might experience when it encounters a moth with two owl-like eyes on its wings, or a caterpillar with two antennal-like tails at its rear end. There are many insects that appear to be composite creatures, the satyrs, centaurs, chimaeras and griffons of the natural world. I decided to call them satyric mimics, because the analogy of a creature that was ambiguous, part human, part goat, seemed most appropriate. I have since realised that the ambiguity is not always built on a simple alternative. Like the chimaera it can involve several, and 'chimaeric' mimicry would be a better term but 'satyric' is now in the scientific literature and it is too late to change it.

The original definition of surrealism as an art form, by André Breton, was a means of revealing the "true intentions of the mind". Breton had worked in a ward with psychiatric patients during the First World War and became interested in Freud's use of dream analysis to unlock the travails of the unconscious mind. He inspired a generation of artists who sought to express a new reality – that which was beyond the 'photographic' image with which we live. This corresponds with Aristotle's concept of *mimesis*, which was not the making of a faithful copy, but a means of isolating the meaning behind the object being copied. To do this, artists such as René Magritte, Max Ernst, Marcel Duchamp and Salvador Dalí produced images, often dreamlike in quality, which are disturbing to us, and to some people even meaningless and repulsive because they seem to throw a spanner into the works of perception, forcing us to examine the nature of reality. As T.S. Eliot remarked in the *Four Quartets* "Human kind cannot bear very much reality." Neither can we bear too much questioning of reality.

It is Magritte particularly who possibly comes closest to representing the anomalies that insect mimics present to us. He shocks us by representing very familiar objects in an unexpected context, as in his portrait of a rose given one of his typically impenetrable titles (*The Wrestlers' Tomb*), and of an apple (*The Listening Room*). Both objects appear to completely fill the small room in which they are portrayed, so you do not know whether, for example, the rose is a normal rose in a room from a doll's house, or a giant artificial rose in a normal-sized room. His ambiguous images include *The Red Model*, a painting of a pair of boots, the lower parts of which transform into feet, and, strangely pertinent to my thesis, *The Companions of Fear*, in which five owls merge seamlessly below their breasts with the large leaves of a plant that looks something like a tobacco plant. These paintings reveal the inspiration for many surrealist advertisements.

We all experience shock when the perceptual logic of the mind is derailed and finishes up on another track. Arthur Koestler in *The Act of Creation* believed that sudden resolution of conflicting interpretations resulted in the release of tension, which is what causes us to laugh at a pun or a conjuring trick. E.H. Gombrich[iv] summed it up as follows:

The experience, common to all, of feeling satisfied that a stick lying in our path is insignificant, only to be suddenly disturbed when it moves and is found in reality to be a snake, brings with it a surprise that can make us

Two ambiguous figures producing visual illusions similar to those presented by the insects on page 109. The figure on the left can be either a young girl or an old woman, while that on the right is seen as either a duck or a rabbit

laugh or cringe. This is symptomatic of the unreliability of perception and the sudden shock, disturbing or pleasurable, that is caused by a change of identity.

There is some evidence that insectivorous birds and other predatory animals similarly experience shock and confusion when they are presented with an ambiguous object or an object in an unexpected context. For the majority of birds and other animals, territory is the most important contextual feature that influences the meaning of a signal. A male robin will viciously attack another male in its territory, flee if it finds itself in another's territory, and sing and display at boundaries of the territory shared with another male. A female bowerbird will respond to the courtship of a male only if he presents himself in front of a well-decorated bower. Our own behaviour is much more greatly influenced by context. This is what Surrealism exploits. Let us revert to the meaning of a red light discussed earlier. On the back of a car, or at traffic lights it means 'stop'. On electronic machinery it usually means 'not functioning', on a heater it generally means 'on'. Outside a house in certain neighbourhoods it has yet another meaning.

Experiments have shown that birds trained to take food from a dish are startled when they are suddenly shown a model of a moth with eye-spots, or even presented with an eye-spot design, or a model of a moth with brightly coloured underwings. And there are numerous descriptive or anecdotal accounts from naturalists of birds in the field being startled by the display of some potential prey insect that suddenly displays bright patches of colour, or eye-spots, or appears to change its form radically.

Biologists of the present generation, however, have been trained in a culture that accepts only evidence that is verifiable statistically, and reject any other form of evidence. While verification of data to support a hypothesis is absolutely vital, science tends to concentrate on this aspect and reject speculation. This, like the antipathy to anthropomorphism, stultifies the acceptance of new ideas and hypotheses. The history of science shows that this has been a recurring theme. The recently released correspondence[v] of Darwin's publisher, John Murray, shows that Murray's

adviser, the Rev. Whitwell Elwin, strongly advised against publication of On _the Origin of Species_, arguing that Darwin's theories were too far-fetched and would never be believed. He wrote: "At every page I was tantalised by the absence of the proofs." The other difficulty here is that any animal behaviourist can usually, though perhaps not knowingly at the time, devise an experiment to give results that support his or her preconceived notions. I have done it myself: 'self-fulfilling prophecies' are more common in experimental science than most people imagine.

The orientation of objects in space relative to ourselves is vastly important to us. This is shown by the illusion on page 113. The brain somehow readjusts the perspective or ignores it in relation to the context. This is analogous is to the problem a translator has. A fault in a sentence (like the one you will find in the previous one if it is read very carefully) may not be apparent if you are reading quickly, but translation into another language means every detail of every word has to be examined separately from the whole sentence, as well as within it.

The Milan fashion company Viktor & Rolf has used inverted imagery to attract attention with great commercial success. They created an upside-down shop window display with chandeliers springing up from the floor and chairs sitting on the ceiling, the whole framing their fashion creations in normal orientation.

Perhaps the greatest testament to the importance of orientation in perception is the iconic piece of surrealist art by Marcel Duchamp, which, in a newspaper poll of five hundred artists, curators, critics and dealers was voted recently the most influential work of art of the twentieth century. In 1917, Duchamp signed his name on a porcelain urinal, which he exhibited turned upside down and named _Fountain_. This familiar structure has become a cornerstone of conceptual art, just because it looks like something else when it is upside down. Like any new departure in art, literature or music, this creation has aroused violent passions. It has been attacked with a hammer twice by Pierre Pinoncelli, a neo-Dadaist, who has also urinated in it. He was arrested and ordered to pay the Pompidou Centre in Paris (where it was last exhibited) 14,000 euros to repair the crack and 200,000 euros for loss in value of the work, a ruling against which he launched an appeal claiming he created a new work of art by damaging it. The court ruling has sparked a vigorous philosophical debate on the value of lavatories, and as the original was lost and the replica is one of eight sanctioned by Duchamp, the Court of Appeal in Paris was left to debate the market value of urinals in the international art market. They finally concluded in February 2007 that Pinoncelli was not liable for the loss in value of the artwork, then valued at over 2.5 million euros.

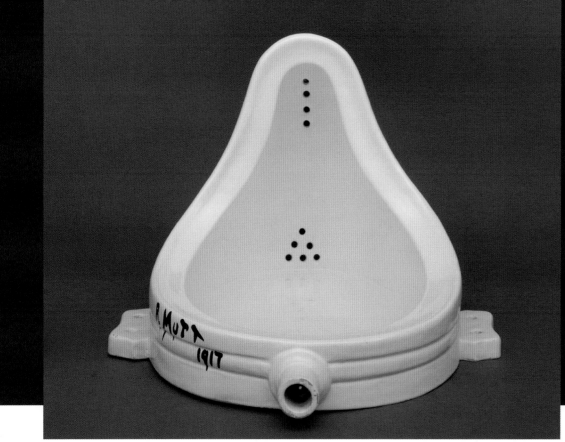

Once again, we find the same dissemblance in nature. The eyed hawk moth in the head-up position on the following page with the fore-wings drawn forwards suggests to us the eyes of two birds peering at us. When viewed with the head down (page 117) it becomes a different creature. The head of a fox reveals itself.

At first it is difficult to see this, but once you have seen it it becomes startlingly clear. Looking at the head of a fox is a useful key to unlock this doorway of perception. A predator, of course, might approach this moth from any orientation. It is our way of ordering the world, seeing things the 'right way up' and not building up an image by assembling the details that makes it difficult for us to see the illusion.

Since our ancestors left the trees in the course of evolution and walked on the ground, the perception of gravity has been a silent judge of the nature of things, as it is, no doubt, for most ground-dwelling vertebrate animals. But most insectivores still forage in the trees, on insects that are also moving about in three-dimensional space, and this has far-reaching consequences for the way they see things.

Most insects are subject to predation by birds and reptiles, and most of these do not have binocular vision. Binocular vision is possible only when the visual fields of the two eyes overlap, but this overlap zone is very small in most birds, with the exception of owls and hawks, which require keen eyesight. In a pigeon the overlap zone is only 1°-2° directly in front of the head, while an owl has binocular vision over about 60° and, like us, has no visual field behind the head. All-round vision is valuable – vital even – like a radar screen, for detecting approaching predators, so why sacrifice it for binocular vision? The reason is that much more information about an object can be abstracted from the zone of overlap of the two eyes. The distance of the object from the observer is more easily deduced from its relative motion and its size. Close one eye and you find yourself in a world that seems two-dimensional. Try touching the tips of your fingers together; it is difficult because you cannot accurately judge the distance of each. People who are blind in one eye can adapt with time and make use of other subtle cues, but these occasionally fail them – as with friend of mine who plays good tennis but occasionally misses the ball by a wide margin.

If you have monocular vision, it is difficult to judge whether you are looking at a small object close to you or a larger object at a distance, because both may subtend the same angle to the eye. What helps the judgment is to make comparisons with the apparent size of other familiar

objects in your visual field, but that delays your perception. The consequence is that a small insect close by will appear to most birds and lizards similar to a larger version further away, and if that insect is a mimic of a snake or a scorpion, for example, its appearance gives it some protection, regardless of its size.

When in Wonderland, Alice had no problems in recognising the creatures around her, despite the fact that she telescoped in and out in size, and neither did Gulliver in his travels. E.H. Gombrich[vi] invited people to do a simple experiment with a bathroom mirror. This involves waiting until there is sufficient condensation on the mirror to partially obscure your image, and then drawing with your finger around the outline of your face. When you then clear the area within the outline you see that this is only about half the size of your actual head. Obviously, even with good binocular vision, the features of an image are far more important to recognition than its size. In the human sphere, the overriding importance of the features is demonstrated in the peculiar illusions grouped under the neologism *pareidolia* in which illusory images are accepted as images that are 'real', and in fact become delusions.

In 1996, in a store called *Bongo Java* in Nashville, a cinnamon bun was produced in which people saw a likeness of Mother Teresa. The fame of this 'miraculous' object spread very rapidly

and the bun was featured in the national press and on television. Eventually this came to the attention of Mother Teresa's lawyer, who objected to the use of the term 'Mother Teresa's cinnamon bun', which had been used in merchandising. The store then trademarked 'NunBun' and 'Immaculate Confection'. Later, Mother Teresa herself became unhappy about money being made from her image, and after discussions with her lawyer the store agreed to use neither Mother Teresa's name nor 'Immaculate confection' on any merchandise. When the lawyer went further and claimed that it was illegal to use the image of the NunBun because it was Mother Teresa's image, the store managers countered by proposing that if it really was her image it would indeed be a miracle, which would support the case for her beatification, and the issue needed to be investigated. There, it appears, the matter has rested, and in the meantime the bun has been stolen.

The NunBun is not, of course, an isolated case of imaginative reconstruction of a visual image, but what it teaches us very clearly is that some people, at least, believe that they are looking at a true image of a Saint to the extent that they are willing to treat it as an icon and pay reverence to it – and pay money for it also. The same applies to the image of the Virgin Mary found on a grilled cheese sandwich, which eventually sold for 28,000 dollars on eBay, and of

The same moth as on pages 114-115, but now the image of a fox's head becomes visible. Looking at the photo of the fox first will make this more apparent

Jesus on a tortilla in New Mexico. The tortilla was put into a shrine where thousands came to pray. In the Islamic world, Arabic inscriptions of the name Allah have appeared on rocks, fish eggs, and so forth, and have similarly occasioned due reverence.

In the case of the NunBun, many people are able to arrive at two different interpretations of an object, and for those who are not swayed to one extreme by religious fervour this can be very amusing. John Kruschke[vii] commented in an Internet article:

> "The fact that two such opposites – Mother Teresa, who aided thousands of starving people, and a cinnamon bun, blithely consumed by the well-fed – can be seen in the same image, only goes to show how ambiguous perception is. The very fact that the two perceptual interpretations are such contradictions is what underlies the humor."

What we also learn from this example is that relative size takes a back seat to analysis of form in the perceptive process. When we look at a death's head hawk moth we are tempted to accept that it has a skull marked on its thorax, even though the image is indistinct, small, and on an insect – one of the last places you would expect to see a skull. The parallel with the NunBun is obvious.

A remarkable example exploiting the irrelevance of the size judgment is found in the chrysalis of a blue butterfly, *Spalgis epius*, which carries the design of the head of a macaque monkey, and is known as the 'ape-fly'. The chrysalis has clearly identifiable marks for eyes, nose, mouth, cheeks, and forehead. Although it is only 5-6 mm long, farmers in West Africa regard this creature with great superstition. This is unfortunate, because the caterpillar is one of the few carnivorous ones, and feeds on mealy bugs, waxy aphid-like insects that are serious crop pests in the tropics. M.G. Venkatesha and his colleagues at Bangalore University observed insectivorous warblers that come to feed on the mealy bugs and claim that the birds are deterred from feeding on the chrysalids.[viii] Thus there are only two possible explanations for the monkey's face. Either it is purely coincidental that the chrysalis takes that form, or natural selection has made it that way because birds and lizards without good distance perception perceive a monkey, in a parallel way to you or I seeing a head in a cinnamon bun.

There are many caterpillars that have appearances as surreal as any of Salvador Dalí's creations, but perhaps nothing is as bizarre as the caterpillar of the lobster moth. This insect is as indecipherable

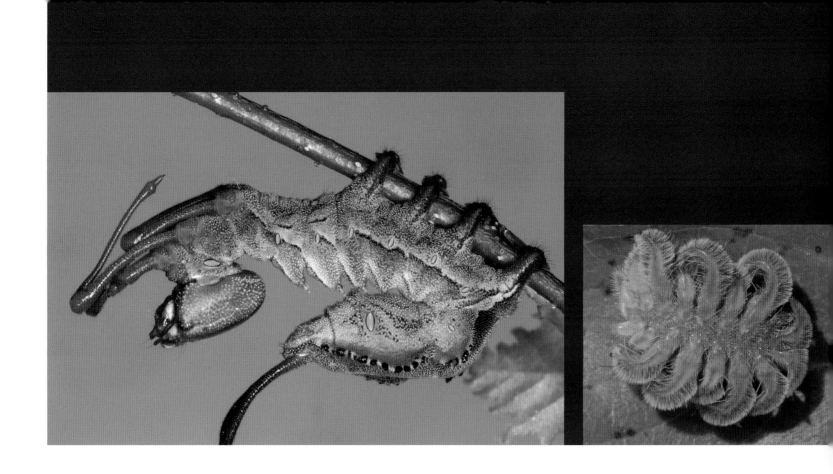

as any of the artist's dream pictures, until it is deconstructed. The young caterpillar is black and has three pairs of very long jointed legs (the true legs), bearing an unmistakable resemblance to an ant. When it is larger, the caterpillar is pale brown and is said to resemble a lobster, from which the moth gets its name. To my eye, the only possible inference of a lobster is in the long, thin-jointed, stick-like front legs. Whoever first named this caterpillar cannot have ever seen a real lobster. Hugh Newman, in his book *British Moths and Their Haunts* describes it thus:

> *"It is almost a beefsteak red with a ridged back like some prehistoric monster, while the whole of the hind portion is flattened and somewhat resembles the expanded head of an angry cobra. When touched or alarmed it will bend back this tail portion of its body while at the same time rearing up its front parts and waving its abnormally long legs in a threatening manner."*

The fact that the caterpillar is reddish in colour makes it more like a cooked lobster than a live one, but what Newman fails to mention is that the last pair of false legs are modified to give the appearance of a bifid tongue, adding credence to an image of a snake head at one end of the body. What is also striking is that this 'head' is very similar indeed to the last bulbous segment of a scorpion's tail, which contains the sting. The sting of a scorpion, furthermore, is a sharply curved barb. At the other end, the rounded head with waving legs is very indicative of a spider. This caterpillar is doubly ambiguous, and perhaps triply so, the whole ensemble of deception suggesting a spider with snake and scorpion features.

Scorpions are among the most feared of animals, and their importance to man is testified by their inclusion in the ancient Egyptian pantheon in association with the goddess Selket, and with Isis who possessed the power to overcome the sting of scorpions. Hundreds of thousands of people are stung by scorpions every year in Mediterranean countries, and although fatalities are far fewer than one in a thousand, the symptoms of a sting are very unpleasant. In earlier times in Egypt they were probably more common than they are now, and an ever-present danger to people.

Clinical information on the effects of a scorpion sting mentions nausea, vomiting, profuse sweating, irritability, salivation, priapism, urinary retention, hyperperistalsis, goose-flesh, convulsions, coma, hypertension, and, in severe cases, symptoms of a heart attack, difficulty in breathing and shock.[ix]

opposite above: **Chrysalis of the ape-fly (*Spalgis epius*), a blue butterfly found in South-East Asia. A similar species occurs in Africa**

above left: **Caterpillar of the lobster moth (*Stauropus fagi*) with elongated forelegs and a bulbous head that resemble the legs and body of a large spider. Viewed upside down, the swollen terminal abdominal segments are seen more clearly to resemble both a snake's head with teeth and forked tongue and the bulbous sting of a scorpion**

above right: **Caterpillar of the hag moth (*Phobetron pithecium*), called the 'monkey slug'. The leg-like appendages covered with urticating hairs bear a close resemblance to a cast tarantula skin**

It is perhaps not surprising that there are relatively few scorpion and spider mimics in the insect world, because a winged insect would have to undergo a huge transformation to look like one. There are a few, such as scorpion flies (Mecoptera), the devil's coach-horse beetle, which arches mock stings over its back, and there exists an extraordinary caterpillar in North America, known as the monkey slug, which bears a startling resemblance to the cast skin of a tarantula spider, the genuine skin of which has hairs which still contain traces of poison. The leg-like appendages of the caterpillar bear similar urticating hairs.

One of the commonest butterflies in the world is the painted lady, *Cynthia cardui*. Focus on the dark parts of the wings and the image of a large spider emerges, as if seen against a background of the sun setting through thorn bushes. Once you have seen this, it is difficult not to see it a second time.

Sometimes the tables are turned, and it is the adult insect that assumes a caterpillar disguise. You might think immediately that this cannot be an advantage to the butterfly because it would attract insectivores rather than repelling them, so two intriguing possibilities arise. The caterpillar image may present a case of satyric mimicry, or the adult may be mimicking the caterpillar.

Why should it do that? Butterflies that are unpalatable are thus because the caterpillars from which they are made sequester toxins from the plants on which they feed. A caterpillar image on the wing border, which is found in many butterflies, could therefore act as a deterrent to experienced insectivores. This suggests the bizarre situation of an insect mimicking the young of its own species! A striking example of this is provided by the magpie moth, *Abraxas grossulariata*, which is rejected by birds, in which the pattern on the caterpillar is replicated on the wings of the moth.

Experiment has shown that insectivorous birds tend to reject caterpillars that are spiny, irrespective of their palatability otherwise, and images of spiny caterpillars are often detectable on the wing margins of adult butterflies. Examples are found in two species of tropical butterfly, the two-tailed pasha (*Charaxes jasius*) and the orange dog swallowtail (*Papilio cresphontes*), which have the border of the underwings in the shape of a caterpillar, with the forelegs of the caterpillar represented by small spikes on the wing, followed by a dark spot marking the caterpillar's head. Depending on the orientation, a bird's bead can also be seen in the *Charaxes*.

Likenesses of spiders and their allies are easily created by images of long, black, curved limbs. While at a conference in Florida on fruit flies – not the tiny *Drosophila* that are used in genetic studies, but the big ones, like Mediterranean fruit fly, that are serious horticultural pests – I was watching a film of the walnut fruit fly, in which the insects were patrolling walnut leaves as part of their courtship ritual. After a few minutes I thought I was hallucinating because I saw jumping spiders instead. Then I realised that the black markings on the transparent wings of the flies figured exactly the legs of a spider. These 'legs' were pointing backwards on the fly, so the illusion came into play only when the insects circled backwards (which they frequently did) moving in a jerky fashion, like spiders.

This gives a clue to the likely function of the stripes on the fore-wings of many swallowtail butterflies. When the insect is in a natural position it has the ends of the legs of huge spiders splayed across its wings. When it is in the set position, the illusion is lost. A similar apparition of a spider can be seen, not only in the painted lady butterfly already mentioned, but in a number of tropical nymphalid species. Once seen, like many visual illusions, it is forever difficult to ignore.

above: **The two-tailed pasha butterfly (*Charaxes jasius*). Rotating the figure reveals a bird's head with gaping beak. Rotating it again reveals a caterpillar-like image on the border of the wing, with typical segmentation and caterpillar spines on the head. It could also be perceived as a spiny grasshopper resting on bark. Compare it with the figure of the caterpillar opposite**

opposite above: **Caterpillar of a nymphalid butterfly.**

opposite below: **The painted lady butterfly (*Cynthia cardui*), which bears the image of a long-legged spider traced across its wings**

In the forests of South and Central America, there is a curious chimaeric creature known as the lantern bug, which has been described as having the head of a serpent, wings of a butterfly, and body of a cicada. It became known as the lantern bug because it was believed to emit light from its grotesque head. The Dutch naturalist Maria Sybilla Merian was one of the first to record this. She was an artist, born in Switzerland in the eighteenth century, who became enthralled with tropical nature and travelled to what was then Dutch Guyana to make illustrations of animals and plants from nature. Her book on the *Metamorphoses of the Insects of Surinam*, a beautifully illustrated folio first published in Dutch in 1705, made her famous in Europe, bringing neotropical biology to the attention of Europeans and introducing them to the lantern bug or *porte-lanterne*. Some Indians brought her a box one day containing the bugs. Awoken in the night by a noise, she took a candle and opened the box containing the bugs. She found that they were all glowing in the dark.

Why those lantern bugs were luminescent has remained a mystery. The only time that luminescence appears to have been recorded since is in insects infected with bioluminescent bacteria, which must be a very rare event. Perhaps Merian's box of bugs also contained some fireflies or other bioluminescent insects but, whatever the reason, this report added to the mystique surrounding this insect, which was named *Fulgora laternaria* by Linnaeus. Fulgora was a goddess of the ancient Romans who protected houses against lightning and fire.

The head is in fact a hollow extension, about the size of a peanut shell, with markings of the teeth, nostrils and eyes of a caiman. It is regarded with as much superstition and dread as the death's head hawk moth. Two scientists, Costa-Neto and Pacheco,[x] went into the native village

The borders of the underwings of the giant swallowtail, or orange dog (*Papilio cresphontes*) appearing as two large caterpillars, which become visible in the head-down position of the butterfly

of Pedra Branca in Bahia, Brazil, and surveyed the perceptions of the indigenous people about this diminutive monster. They found that the fear and aversion to this insect were due to its bizarre collection of features, which besides the alligator head included large 'eagle-owl' eye-spots on the hind wings, apparent absence of mouth and eyes, loose white wax flakes over the body, and a 'sting'. The sting is in fact the piercing proboscis that is found on all true bugs, and with which they penetrate leaves and stems to obtain sap from trees. However, this 'sting' was assumed to be venomous, lethal to trees, humans and animals. When the insect is disturbed, it drums its head on the tree trunk, emits a foul smell, and flies away displaying its owl eyes.

The two biologists then asked the village people to say what they thought the creature was. The replies were very revealing, bearing in mind that these were people close to nature who needed to make judgements about animals and plants in order to survive, and were not educated in modern systems of classification. It was recognised as a dangerous and potentially lethal animal. It was classified by 37 per cent as a snake, 4 per cent as a butterfly, 3 per cent as a cicada, 2 per cent as a beetle and 1 per cent as a cricket.

The common name used throughout Brazil for the lantern bug is *Jequitiranaboia*. According to Evaldo Costa-Neto this comes from the Tupi-guarani language, the name reflecting the ambiguity of the insect. *Yeki* means cicada, *rana* is a frog, and *mboya* is a snake. Other names used in the Amazon region of Brazil can be translated as winged snake, flying reptile, cricket-snake, caiman-snake, crazy cicada. Close examination shows that although the similarities with the head of a caiman are there, there are also features of the venomous pit vipers, shown, for example, by the black spot on the side of the false head, which recalls the heat-sensitive pit organ of these snakes.

left: **Caterpillar of a giant silk moth**

top right: **The apple maggot fruit fly, a pest of apples in the USA, with wing markings that portray the legs of a hunting spider**

bottom right: **The tiger swallowtail butterfly (*Papilio glaucus*) with wing markings that resemble the legs of large spiders**

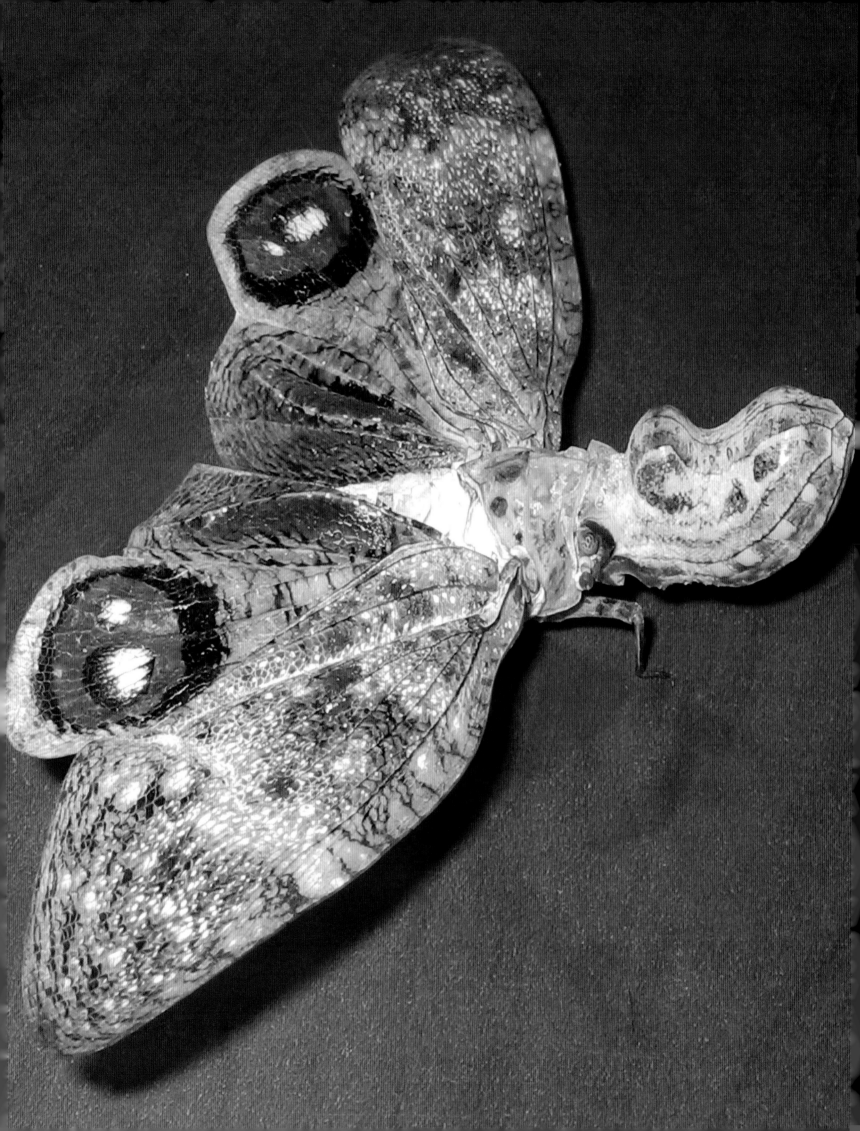

This gives us a fascinating insight into the ways that ambiguous animals are perceived. The lantern bug is seen as a dangerous and venomous creature both because it is a chimaera and because it has visual features of poisonous snakes built into it. At one level it produces hesitation and at another it provokes fear. It would be surprising if its animal predators such as birds, monkeys and reptiles did not recognise it in a similar way.

Humans respond in rather unexpected ways. In many places in Latin America the bug is known as the *machaca*, which literally means a crusher and presumably refers to the supposed power of the insect. In Colombia, someone with a large sexual appetite is said to be *picada por la machaca* – stung by the lantern bug. There is a story that some fifty years ago two journalists went to visit a remote village in Colombia to report on an annual religious festival. They arrived a day late, and wandered around the artisan market looking for an alternative subject to report on. On one stall they found a *machaca* and asked what it was. The stall owner explained that it was used as an amulet, symbolising potency, but if someone was bitten by such a creature the bite was fatal, and the only remedy was to have sexual intercourse (preferably with a virgin) within twenty-four hours. This curiosity was reported in the newspaper, and there was a sudden epidemic of *machaca* bites among young men. Monks in a nearby monastery decided to risk death rather than submit to the cure, but it is believed that many people owed their marriage to this myth. Many tribes in Latin America carry lantern bugs in their bags of amulets, a reflection of what has been called the 'terrifying powers' of the insects.

Entomologists have always been bemused by the caiman image of the lantern bug and have questioned whether the interpretation is correct. What would a caiman only a few inches long – and only its head at that – be doing high on a tree-trunk? The same question could be asked of the image on the wings of moths. This question arises out of our anthropocentricity, because the head, to our perception, is imperfect, incomplete, and in a totally unexpected context. There are a number of answers that are more easily provided if we imagine how a bird or reptile sees it.

opposite: **The lantern bug (*Fulgora laternaria*)**

above: **A dwarf caiman**

Snake
Icons

"He thought he saw a Rattlesnake
That questioned him in Greek,
He looked again and found it was
The Middle of Next Week
'The one thing I regret,' he said,
'Is that it cannot speak!'"

Lewis Carroll: *Sylvie and Bruno*

I have already questioned the idea that Batesian mimicry will be successful only if the predators survive, because the learnt aversion is what protects what would otherwise be their prey. Starting from this point it is usually argued that insects would not become mimics of other animals that are lethal, such as snakes, scorpions, alligators, monkeys and so on, because an insectivorous animal attempting to feed on one of these would not live to tell the tale. A little reflection shows that this is a rather arbitrary assumption.

The argument goes something like this: if a bird walks up to a snake, it will not be able to pass on to its offspring the information that this is not a safe thing to do. Since birds cannot learn this through experience, they will only increase their chances of survival if they have an innate aversion to snake-like objects. But there is no good evidence that they do have that, so there is no point in an insect mimicking a snake. End of story.

We know intuitively that this argument is, at the very least, tendentious. People are afraid of snakes, scorpions, wasps, lions, etc., and, even if they have never seen a live snake or scorpion before, they can develop phobias that interfere with their lives. Reputation alone is enough to establish a phobia. Why, then, preclude the possibility that animals can be frightened by the same venomous creatures, or iconic representations of them, when they have never been attacked by them previously and may even never have seen them before?

There has been much argument about whether fear of snakes is part of our genetic inheritance; studies by different people having yielded differing conclusions. Ramona and Desmond Morris[i] have described the results of a survey that was done through the medium of a children's television programme. They asked questions like, "Which animal do you dislike most?" The snake came top, selected by 27 per cent of 11,960 children. This fear appears to develop around the age of four, but by the age of fourteen the percentage affected fell below 20 per cent. A similar study on fears and phobias carried out in New England by psychologists revealed that 38 per cent of females and 12 per cent of males considered snakes the most fearful animals.[ii]

In the Palaeolithic period, there are reasons to believe that the moon was seen as a goddess. The lunar cycles parallel and appear to control so many aspects of the natural world, including the seasons and the fertility of animals and man. As Baring and Cashford[iii] put it, "The moon died and came to life again; the serpent sloughed its skin yet remained alive," and so the snake became a symbol of death and rebirth. The earliest signs of the snake are thus serpentine engravings on bones and on cave walls. But the other animals that figure in cave art, apart from

BUTTERFLIES Messages from Psyche

those that were hunted, such as bison, deer and mammoths, were the lion and the owl. These, like snakes, were ubiquitous and fear-provoking, and so formed part of the primitive pantheon of gods in many parts of the world, with the jaguar or puma replacing the lion in the New World.

The snake, as we are informed in the Book of Genesis, deceived Eve into eating the fruit from the tree of knowledge of good and evil in the Garden of Eden, after which God banished Adam and Eve, leaving them to survive as best they could. God cursed the snake, saying:

> "I will put enmity between you and the woman, and between your offspring and hers; he will crush your head, and you will strike his heel."

Another reference to snakes in the Bible[iv] concerns the contest that Moses and Aaron had with snake charmers that the Pharaoh provided. When the Pharaoh asked them to perform a miracle, as God had instructed Aaron, he threw down his staff and it became a snake.

> "Pharaoh then summoned the wise men and sorcerers, and the Egyptian magicians also did the same thing by their own secret arts: Each one threw down his staff and it became a snake. But Aaron's staff swallowed up all the other staffs."

Of course, Pharaoh took it badly when his team lost, and Egypt suffered the seven plagues for his subsequent intransigence. The origin of this story probably lies in the fact that snake charmers can induce a catatonic state in a snake, similar to hypnosis, by applying pressure behind the head. The rod-like snake then appears to come into life again when thrown upon the ground.

This biblical account points to the fact that snakes were an ever-present hazard in the daily lives of the ancient Egyptians. In the Middle Kingdom, snakes were engraved on knives and apotropaeic (magic) wands, which were used, in conjunction with spells, to repel venomous snakes from the bedrooms of expectant mothers and mothers with babies.

The snake that figures most widely in the mythology of the Mediterranean and Asian countries is the cobra, which exists as several closely-related species. Cobras, which can grow to a length of two metres, distinguish themselves by the ability to rear up when provoked, expanding the flesh in the collar region to form the hood, which has two large eye-spots on its upper surface.

The story of the serpent in the Garden of Eden is just one of many accounts in the history of art, religious texts and folklore that identifies the snake as an evil creature, a kind of devil in both ancient and contemporary religions. On the other hand, various deities have become associated with snakes, especially with the cobra. This first came to my attention when I was studying the termite fauna in southern India. There, one occasionally comes across a termite mound that has been decorated with paint, flowers and garlands, and has a bowl of food placed on it. Such mounds have become shrines to the king cobra, the *Naja* of Hindu religious mythology, which has a god-like status. It often makes a home for itself in the subterranean ventilation shafts of abandoned termite mounds. The cobra is one of the most venomous snakes and a bite can result in death within an hour. There are reputedly thousands of deaths every year from cobra bites in India, but thousands are kept by snake charmers. They are often rendered harmless by removal of their poison fangs with the consequence that they cannot feed properly and ultimately die, but if a venomous cobra enters someone's house it will often be tolerated because of its religious associations.

The Hindu Lord of Creation, Nataraja, has a snake coiled round him. This symbolises the power he has over what is regarded as the most dangerous animal. It is said that the Hindus see moulting of the skin by snakes as an allegorical representation of death and rebirth in a new body. Vishnu, the preserver of the Universe, is usually portrayed as reclining on the coiled body of Sheshnag, the pre-eminent serpent, a giant snake deity with multiple cobra heads.

Fear of snakes seems to support Jung's view that we are born with archetypes in the mind that influence our perception without us being fully aware of it. Snakes figure in the mythology of societies throughout the world, adding weight to this view. In Minoan Crete two figurines were found which have been interpreted variously as representing either a snake goddess or a priestess of a snake cult. The women of Troy also wore headdresses with snake ornaments on them,

sometimes with a snakehead at the front.[v] As for the Hindus, it is likely that here the snake represented the power of women in societies that were essentially peaceful. By accident or design, this same symbolic use of a snake's head on the forehead found its way to the Egyptians.

Much argument surrounds the issue of the development of behaviour and what is instinctive and what is learnt. This happens because behaviour can only develop in response to what is in the environment, and an animal cannot be separated from some sort of experience that might determine how it responds to something else later. So the jury is likely to stay out forever on the instinct or learning dichotomy.

It has been mooted[vi] that fear of reptiles is genetically inherited and ingrained in the human psyche as a result of evolutionary processes affecting our remote ancestors. Snakes and certain other reptiles such as crocodiles and alligators, because of the threat they posed, would thus have accumulated special psychological significance over the course of evolution for both humans and other primates. *Homo sapiens* is believed to have emerged in Africa some two hundred thousand years ago, while other humanoids have been in existence for over ten million years.

Wittgenstein made the famous remark that if a lion could talk, we would not be able to understand him. The major difference between us and other primates is that they do not have the vocal apparatus that we do and so can produce only a small range of sounds. We can only speculate on whether this limitation in their ability to communicate restricted the development of their brains and cognitive ability – but this is in any case a chicken and egg problem. In 1980 Robert Cheney and Dorothy Seyforth[vii] published their research on the calls of vervet monkeys in the Amboseli game park in Kenya and provoked a new wave of interest (and controversy) in the study of the evolution of human speech. They identified three types of warning calls that were given by the monkeys to what were evidently their most feared enemies: snakes, eagle owls, and leopards. These monkeys react very strongly to snakes they encounter, screaming at them and darting to and fro. In response to the snake call, they rear up on their hind legs and search the grassland around them. In reply to the eagle owl call, they gather close to the trunk of a tree or go into thorn bushes, and on hearing the leopard call, they climb into the branches of the nearest tree where the leopard is unlikely to follow. Wild chimpanzees and baboons also have a number of call types;[viii] the most easily recognised one is the bark given to a snake.

Desmond Morris was able to do some simple tests with primates when he was Director of London Zoo. He and his wife tested the responses of chimpanzees and other apes to snake-like

objects. After several years of living with a young chimpanzee reared as a baby, they took away a piece of rubber tubing he was playing with, painted zigzag snake-like markings on it and gave it back.

> *"He retreated, then advanced with all his hair on end and dealt it a vicious blow just behind its 'head'. No sooner was the blow struck than the animal was leaping back out of the way."*

Ramona and Desmond Morris also describe an experience with two orang-utans. These were used in TV programmes that he presented.

> *"Also reared in captivity from tiny babies, they accidentally saw a tame python in a television studio one day. They were up the wall and into the studio rigging quicker than they had ever moved before in their lives."*

Two psychologists, Arne Oehman and Susan Mineka, found that although monkeys generally were fearful of snakes and responded to them with alarm calls, mobbing, and avoidance, fear was much less common among monkeys reared in captivity.[x] The two psychologists carried out conditioning experiments with laboratory reared monkeys, which showed that monkeys showing initial indifference to snakes acquired a fear of them by watching a wild-reared monkey reacting to live and toy snakes. This is obviously very like the way in which children develop phobias of spiders and other 'creepy-crawlies' by taking on board their mother's alarm. However, Oehman and Mineka found that while it was easy to condition (train) monkeys to fear snakes, it was almost impossible to condition them to avoid rabbits or flowers. It seems that in primates there is an inherited predisposition to learn about certain things that may be life threatening.

There is also evidence that fear of bright colour patterns is instinctive. It has been shown that birds that have been bred in captivity are alarmed when they are presented with sticks painted with the red, black and yellow rings that typify a coral snake, even though they had never seen a snake. This may just be a case of bright colours attracting attention or it may be that animals other than primates rely upon fast-track information processing alone, having no well-developed cerebral hemispheres to review different interpretations of what they are seeing. It has been shown that when humans who have no fear of snakes are shown them, there is an

above left: **A shrine to the king cobra in southern India, formed from an old termite mound in which the snake is living**

above right: **The 'Snake Goddess', a statue of a priestess from Knossos, possibly connected with a snake cult of Minoan Crete, c.1600 BC. Archaeological Museum, Herakleion**

immediate physiological reaction detectable as a skin response that occurs in the absence of any overt reaction. The immediate perception thus appears to be subliminal.

Some years ago, I accompanied an expedition to film the animals of the Emas National Park on the edge of the Mato Grosso in Brazil. I went with the producer, Richard Matthews, and a cameraman, Martin, in a narrow boat to film along the river that runs through the park. Unfortunately, there was no map of the area to rely on, only an aerial photograph. Largely as a result of this, we considerably underestimated the time to reach the agreed pick-up point downstream, and as darkness came on, the boat capsized in a narrow passage in the narrow strip of forest. We managed to struggle out of the water and found ourselves in a swampy forest in the dark with a faltering torch and a compass. It took us five hours wading through mud and pushing through bushes and creepers to reach dry land, where a rescue vehicle was waiting. Richard, who I thought was fearless and was inured to tropical hazards, having seen him the day before filming a giant anaconda at close range, later wrote in his book *Nightmares of Nature* that this was the most terrifying experience he had ever had, because of fear of snakes. Every step we took in the dark carried the danger of a snake bite, and we all knew the risk we were taking.

Estimates show that about five million people a year suffer from snake bites. There are a thousand fatalities a year in Africa, three thousand in Brazil, Ecuador and Venezuela. India and Pakistan suffer eight thousand deaths, and the Middle East twenty thousand. In Brazil there are one and a half to two thousand a month, with 90 per cent of bites by venomous snakes from the *fer-de-lance* or lancehead, 9 per cent from bushmasters and less than 1 per cent from coral snakes. However, the two latter are the most venomous, and without treatment mortality is 72 per cent and 100 per cent respectively, against 8 per cent for the *fer-de-lance*.

I began this chapter by saying that the tacit assumption that there is no profit in being a mimic of a venomous animal is obviously a false one. To begin with, biologists readily accept that wasps and hornets are common models, presumably because a predator is likely to survive a single sting. Nevertheless, the chances of being killed by molesting a snake are not always high. Not all snakes are venomous, some are only weakly so, and just the strike from a snake can be

very frightening. Surprisingly, there is really no name in common scientific parlance for this kind of mimicry, which is a form of masquerade. The following extract is from World Health Organisation advice on the treatment of snake bites in South-East Asia:

> *"Some people, who are bitten by snakes or suspect or imagine that they have been bitten, may develop quite striking symptoms and signs, even when no venom has been injected. This results from an understandable fear of the consequences of a real venomous bite. Anxious people may overbreathe so that they develop pins and needles of the extremities, stiffness or tetany of their hands and feet and dizziness. Others may develop vasovagal shock after the bite or suspected bite – faintness and collapse with profound slowing of the heart."*

Descriptions of the pathological effects of the bite of a poisonous snake that is not quickly treated are not for the faint-hearted; in extreme circumstances tissue necrosis, destruction of the bone marrow, kidney damage and brain damage can result. The psychological effect can also be potentially lethal. A French colleague once told me of a dockworker in Dieppe who had collapsed after being bitten by a snake. Someone realised that it was important to identify the snake before giving anti-venom and phoned the Zoology Department of the University of the Sorbonne. It was late in the day and that was closed, but they managed to get the home telephone number of the Professor of Zoology. Unfortunately, he turned out to be a specialist in the study of marine plankton, but he drove through the night to the port, where the docker was starting to go into heart failure and a priest had been sent for. A brief examination confirmed that the 'snake' was a large eel.

There are caterpillars that are obvious snake mimics, although they may be much smaller than the average snake. The caterpillar of the elephant hawk moth is an example. Every summer, when I was working in the biology department of my university, I would get telephone calls from people who had found this weird creature with two 'eyes' at the front of its head. "Is it a snake?" was always the question. If the average person can be deceived, or have grave doubts about a harmless caterpillar, we should not be surprised if the average bird has difficulty too.

above: **Caterpillar of a swallowtail butterfly with its forked tongue-like osmaterium everted**

opposite left: **The fully-grown caterpillar of the elephant hawk moth (*Deilephila elpenor*) showing the segments behind the head that can be inflated to suggest a false head with prominent eyes**

opposite right: **Close-up of the elephant hawk moth caterpillar with the false head inflated**

The snake effect is accentuated by the elephant hawk caterpillar inflating the segments behind the head to make the eye-spots more prominent, and by making brusque striking movements with its head.

While a snake can be identified because it is long and thin, and has two eyes, the other feature that signifies it is the red or yellow forked tongue, which is flicked in and out to 'taste' odour by trapping odour molecules on the tongue surface. The caterpillars of swallowtail butterflies have a similar 'tongue' which they protrude by inflating it from behind the head. This is usually bright yellow or orange and is known as an *osmaterium*. It is more than just a visual signal, it is a glandular structure that produces in some species a pungent and repellent odour of rancid butter (butyric acid). This acid is toxic to ants, but, perhaps not coincidentally, some species of snake produce similar odours as a form of defence against *ophidophagous* snakes (snakes that eat other snakes).

The caterpillar of the puss moth has at its tail end a forked 'tongue', which it can shoot out like the double tail of a kite. When alarmed it presents a terrifying image, inflating its head, which has two eye-spots in a red-ringed face, and flicking forward its forked appendage, which can also discharge salicylic acid, the acid that forms the basis of aspirin, and protects the willow trees, on which the caterpillar feeds, from other herbivores. Viewed from the front, the image resembles an open-mouthed reptile with concealed jaws. This insect is also chimaeric. The three pairs of true legs are striped yellow and black, so that when they are gripping a plant stem this banded pattern is visible from below, producing a crude image of a wasp's abdomen.

Brightly coloured butterflies with black, red and yellow, or orange wings are found everywhere in the tropical forests of South and Central America. Many of these are the passion vine butterflies, or Heliconids, slow flying and apparently immune to almost all predators. In *Travels on the Amazon and Rio Negro* Wallace noted that

> "In the Brazilian forests there are great numbers of insectivorous birds – as jacamars, trogons, and puffbirds – which catch insects on the wing … and the wings of those insects are often found on the ground where their bodies have been devoured. But among these there are no wings of Heliconidae."

Thomas Belt, who travelled in Nicaragua during the same period told the Royal Entomological Society that he had observed a pair of puffbirds catching butterflies for half an hour, but they never brought back any of the heliconids that were flying about lazily in great numbers, and

Three passion vine butterflies (*Heliconius melpomene*), all Müllerian mimics and each a different sub-species. Other species occur which share the same basic pattern, adding to mimicry rings

which could have been captured more easily than all the rest. He also had a tame white-faced monkey that was extremely fond of insects, but would never touch passion vine butterflies:

"He was too polite not to take them when they were offered to him, and would sometimes smell them, but invariably rolled them up in his hand and dropped them quietly again after a few moments."

Among the Aztecs, butterflies were sometimes regarded as symbols of fire, because of what has been described as the 'conflagration of colour' produced when they flew in a cloud.[xi] This must be a reference to passion vine butterfly mimicry rings, which are common in Mexico. The members of the mimicry ring are, of course, a mixture of Müllerian and Batesian mimics, each species benefiting from the reputation of others in their mixed society.

During my visits to Brazil, I have seen many astonishingly beautiful animals and plants, but the highlight of my experiences was a walk through a stream in the Mato Grosso with my late friend David Gifford. David, early in his career, had written a guide to the butterflies of Zambia, and when he was invited to head the Ecology Laboratory of the new University of Brasilia in the 1970s, he devoted himself with tireless enthusiasm to collecting and studying the butterfly fauna of central Brazil. He eventually died in his Sisyphean attempts to help conserve some of the unique environments in Brazil.

David wanted to show me a 'mimicry ring' of butterflies: an assemblage of insects all sharing elements of the same colour pattern. We strolled up a shallow stream in the early morning with the sun filtering through the trees and patterning the surface of the water. Suddenly, it seemed as though the dappled light came alive and multiplied into a kaleidoscopic pattern of coloured stars. These were the passion vine butterflies, and their cousins the clearwings, which had broken free from the riverbank, and were dancing over the water catching the sun's rays as they did so.

There are many different species of these passion vine and glass-wing butterflies, the differences between them being slight and often difficult to discern. But in a mimicry ring like this there are also butterflies and other insects from quite distinct and totally unrelated groups. There was a member of the swallowtail family (without tails!) and a member of the whites and yellows, all of which had lost the hallmarks of their families and had evolved to become copies of the passion vine species. Not only that, but there were day-flying moths, and even bugs that were on the same colour bandwagon. Over thirty different species can co-exist in these mimicry rings; they keep together and fly in a strange rainbow cloud of orange, red, yellow and black. David and his fellow entomologist Keith Brown had found hundreds of passion vine butterflies in the state of Roraima, some unique to particular areas, and hence the probability that they may already have been lost in land clearance during the last thirty years is sadly very high.

Further upstream, I learnt another lesson about mimicry. The botanist with us, Dr. Jim Ratter, picked up a large leaf, remarking, "You can eat this. The local Indians use it as a food wrapping in the markets." He started to chew it. After a few minutes, we realised that the usually voluble scientist had fallen totally silent, and was opening his mouth like a freshly landed fish, without any words coming out. Plants can also mimic each other – in their leaf form, and the highly skilled taxonomist had been deceived by a plant that harboured a powerful local anaesthetic!

The passion flower vines (Passifloras) on which the caterpillars feed are themselves masters of the art of mimicry, going to extraordinary lengths to avoid being eaten. The leaves are rich in poisonous cyanides, which are effective defences against all the herbivorous insects around, except for a very few, including the passion vine butterflies that have evolved means of tolerating the poisons which are sequestered in their tissues (mainly in the hardened wings where they cannot easily escape into the bloodstream). The caterpillars are able to detoxify them with the use of enzymes. This puts a big table of food at their disposal, which is out of reach of most of the other congregation of mouths that there are around. In our world, we overcome the toxicity of many vegetable foods by careful preparation. Cassava, for example, is full of cyanides until they

A Texas coral snake
(Micrurus tener), with the red,
black and yellow patterns that
are assumed by many South
American butterflies

A decorative wall hanging
from indigenous tribes in the
Rio Negro (Manaus) with
coral snake designs

have been extracted by soaking in water and further neutralised by cooking. Potato alkaloids, found in the green tissue are potentially lethal but are also are destroyed by cooking. On the other hand, our susceptibility to alcohol, another common poison, is very low because of enzymes in the liver that neutralise it.

Passion vine butterflies usually lay eggs on the tendrils of the vine, and to counter this, the plants have evolved special false tendrils that drop off the plant, carrying any eggs to the ground with them. Other tendrils carry a tiny, bright yellow, skittle-shaped protuberance, which is a mimic of the butterfly's egg. This deceives the butterfly into registering that the plant has already been colonised by another female, so potentially limiting the food available for her offspring. This deception is reinforced in some vine species by the stipules (small leaflets at the junctions between the stems), which are curled round into a cylinder with projecting horns and resemble caterpillars.

If so many details of behaviour, evolution, survival and ecology rest upon the passion vine butterflies' coloured costumes, there must be something special about them. Are the butterflies modelling themselves on something that is even more dangerous to other animals than they are? If so, that has to be a venomous snake, and the finger points immediately at the coral snakes.

The bushmasters and lanceheads are cryptically coloured and difficult to spot in the undergrowth. I inadvertently stood on a bushmaster once at the base of a tree. But the coral snakes stand out like traffic lights on the forest floor, revealing flashes of colour when they move through a carpet of leaves. Coral snakes, which also occur as far north as the southern states of the USA, are 2-5 ft. long and strikingly coloured, most commonly with repeated banding in black, red and yellow. These snakes are rarely seen during the day, when they stay in burrows, and their poison fangs are not as efficient as in most other snakes so that in the USA there are few instances of coral snake bites and those that need treatment are effectively dealt with by injection of anti-venom. The venom acts against the respiratory system and paralyses the diaphragm, so that the

victim of a serious bite may need artificial respiration for a week or more. The venom can also have chronic effects on health that persist for weeks after the bite.

Evidence that coral snakes can be anathema to birds appears in one of Audubon's magnificent paintings from *The Birds of America*. His portrait of the bizarrely named chuck-wills-widow, a relative of the nightjar, shows the birds threatening a poisonous coral snake. Audubon observed this directly and heard the birds hissing open-mouthed at the snake, which he wrongly identified as a harmless species. The species he illustrates is in fact a poisonous coral snake, highlighting again the fact that even the most skilled observer and artist cannot easily discriminate between a model and mimic, while birds apparently can do so – at any rate they take no chances.

In tropical South and Central American forests the snake is more readily encountered among the indigenous population, and is less easily dealt with. It is not surprising that the coral snake has a place in the folklore of Amazonian tribes, and designs woven into basket-ware and coarse cloth are found throughout the Amazon region.

In 1976, David Guss travelled to the lower Orinoco to study the creation myths of the Yekuana Indians who live in the Venezuelan Amazon region. Expecting mainly to hear stories passed down from the elders, he found that mythology permeated every aspect of the daily lives of the Yekuana. Vital to the understanding of their society is a tradition of basket weaving; the baskets have in-built symbolism, which makes them a novel and distinctive art form.

In one of their legends, their ancestors steal a box from a huge ferocious monkey. Inside the box are drawings of animals, which are used in the designs of their basketwork. Flat baskets serving as plates, known as *wajas*, are made by the men who use them as a form of expressing their character and feelings in courtship, and after marriage. It has been suggested that they are symbolic maps of their private universe, representing the heavens and also symbols of the environment and animals around them.

Audubon's illustration of the Chuck-Will's-Widow, a relative of the nightjar, threatening a poisonous coral snake

above: **The citrus swallowtail (***Papilio demodocus***) with the image of an open-mouthed snake on the underwings**

opposite above: **The Atlas moth (***Attacus atlas***) from South-East Asia. The snake-heads are clearly visible from both the upper- and undersides, with the coils of the snake body delineated around the edges of the wings. Flicking movements of the wings sometimes help to create the illusion of a snake striking**

opposite right: **The hawk moth *Enyo lugubris*, a bat mimic with abdominal appendages suggesting ears**

Amongst the animals represented on the wajas are the jaguar and the coral snake, the two most feared and powerful animals in their world. Corresponding to the colour pattern of the snakes, the basket weaves are in red and black on a straw-coloured background.

The highly poisonous coral snakes have Batesian mimics, which share the same colour pattern and are difficult to distinguish. In the southern USA there is a rhyme: "Red touch yellow, kill a fellow, Red touch black, venom lack." The north American coral snakes have yellow or white bands enclosing black and red bands alternately – so red and black never touch – while the mimics, which are non-venomous milk snakes and king snakes, have the red bands enclosed either side by black bands. This distinction, though, does not always hold in South America, although in the southern USA it no doubt prevents the destruction of a lot of innocent non-poisonous snakes. This reasoning, however, is not open to potential animal predators, who would have to make a detailed examination to be sure there was no threat to them.

The bright colours of the American coral snakes are typical, as we have seen, of venomous or poisonous animals that need to be highly visible, like advertisements on a billboard, so that they are easily remembered and associated with fear (or pleasure in most advertisements).

While most butterflies of the swallowtail family show features of birds on their wings, as we shall see in Chapter 10, one of the commonest African swallowtails, the citrus swallowtail, *Papilio demodocus*, has the image of an open-mouthed snake on its underwings. This is difficult for us to see unless we look at the insect with the body at about 45° from the horizontal, for reasons we have already examined in the last chapter.

It is among the giant silk moths (Saturniidae) that mimicry of snakes is most common: snake images are to be found on the wing margins. It is curious that they are found only in association with the transparent 'windows' that many of these moths have on their wings,

and moths that have eye-spots on their wings very rarely have windows as well, so there are two separate evolutionary strategies: moths that defend themselves with snake images and windows, and moths that defend themselves with eye-spots.

The outer margin of the fore-wings in the Atlas moth, for example, has a very small eye-spot at the tip. The wingtip is curved outwards and carries a line below the eye-spot. There is thus a crude image of a snake down the outer edges of the wings either side. In its natural pose, the way in which the hind-wings abut against the fore-wings produces the illusion of the coil of the snake's body. The impression of a snake is increased by flicking movements of the wings that the insect makes when it is disturbed, which move the eye-spot round in an elliptical arc like the swaying movement of a snake about to strike. If it is disturbed further, the insect may drop to the ground beating its wings rapidly and then throw itself onto its back and recover onto its feet again, so that the action recalls the rapid uncoiling of a snake.

The Atlas moth, like the death's head hawk moth, has other faces. Now concentrate on the remaining features of the insect in its natural resting position and you see that if you subtract the snake images on each side there is a dark reddish brown zone that can easily be interpreted as the wings of a bat, or a bird about to land. Unsurprisingly, this image is no longer decipherable when the wings are in the set position, and as with many of the examples I have chosen, you cannot see it in the insect in a museum cabinet.

This darker image of outstretched wings is found quite commonly among the giant silk moths, and may be more widespread than we might imagine. In the Amazon I photographed a hawk moth that was well camouflaged amongst the dried leaves of the forest floor, but it was years later when I happened to look at the photograph upside down on my desk that I realised it was, from that view, a mimic of one of the numerous species of bat that roost under large-leaved plants in the Amazon forest.

The Evil Eye

"Though we know rationally that there is no difference in outward appearance between a seeing eye and a blind one and that even a glass eye can reasonably simulate the appearance, I contend it would be false to say that any eye looks like a vitreous sphere. The task of the artist therefore is not necessarily to fashion a facsimile eye. It is to find a way of stimulating the response to a living gaze."

E. H. Gombrich: *Illusion in Nature and Art*

I n modern Chinese the sun is represented by a circle with a spot in the middle, so it suggests an eye, as it does in Egyptian hieroglyphs, where it is a circle within a circle. Both Plato and Shakespeare saw the eye and the sun as one and the same. In *The Republic* Plato says (in dialogue with Glaucon):

"Yet of all the organs of sense the eye is most like the sun?
By far the most like.
And the power which the eye possesses is a sort of effluence which is dispensed from the sun?
Exactly"

While Shakespeare, in his *Sonnets*, fears that his lover may "scarcely greet me with that sun, thine eye."

The eye is probably the most powerful symbol and archetype that we have. One of the most potent figures of ancient Greek mythology is the Medusa, one of three sisters, the Gorgons, who were sea nymphs. Medusa slept with Poseidon in one of Athene's temples. The enraged goddess then turned Medusa into an ugly winged monster with snakes for hair, glaring eyes, large teeth, a protruding tongue, and powerful claws. Her glance turned men to stone.[i] She was eventually killed by Perseus to whom Athene presented a highly polished shield to act as a mirror so that he could avoid looking the Medusa in the eye while delivering the *coup de grâce*.

The eye of the god Horus was also a powerful symbol for the ancient Egyptians. This can be traced to the Egyptian creation myth in which the sun god Ra was the visible manifestation of Atum, who was responsible for the creation of air, light, the sky and the earth. The descendants of the sky goddess and the earth god included Osiris, who was the first king of Egypt, and later became the ruler of the underworld and eternity, Isis, his sister, and Seth his brother and bitter rival. Isis had a son, Horus, who had the head of an Egyptian falcon. Horus fought with Seth, losing his left eye, but emerged as the victor of the contest. He then travelled to the Underworld to see Osiris who had been murdered by Seth, and presented him with his lost eye. The eye revived Osiris who set the seasons into motion again, and it became known as the *Wedjat Eye*, meaning the eye of wholeness and restoration, which was then a talismanic symbol warding off evil.

There are alternative versions of this legend that provide a link to the moon, which in earlier versions was said to be represented by the left eye of Horus (the right representing the sun). For example, one story tells us that the eye was divided into six parts, but was restored by the god

previous page: **The eye-spots of a giant silk-moth (*Antherina suraka*) from Madagascar help to create the impression of a lemur's face**

Thoth and fourteen other gods in six days, the total corresponding to the days leading up to the full moon. While the left eye represented the sun and the moon and healing, the right eye represented the sun's cycle.

The Head of the Gorgon Medusa by Bernini. Capitoline Museum, Rome

Horus was the sunlight, 'piercing the sky like a falcon'. In the New Kingdom, the eye is often presented with wings. The winged eye occurs also in other cultures; for example, in North and Central America, Robin Edgar[ii] has made a convincing argument to link the Wedjat Eye with the appearance of the sun at a total eclipse. His reasoning is that during eclipse the sun appears as a dark disc surrounded by a diffuse bright penumbra, which gives the appearance of wings extending out from a dark pupil. The same phenomenon occurs with a lunar eclipse and so would explain the duality of Horus's eyes. At times of eclipse, it would probably have been thought that the sun (or moon) god or goddess was descending to earth on wings.

The Wedjat Eye was undoubtedly the forerunner of the Evil Eye and the dark pupil representing the sun disk forms only part of that image. The eye symbolises power through association with the falcon, reproducing the eye of the Egyptian falcon and the dark lines around it, with one

curious addition: a line leading down from the tear duct and ending in a scroll. This resembles the tear channel below the eye of a cheetah or lion (in one legend the eye of Ra shed tears from which people developed). The lion-headed goddess Sekhmet represented a source of power and a force for the destruction of evil and illness, so making the eye a more potent combined symbol of the falcon (Horus) and the lion (Sekhmet).

Another possible explanation for the scrolled line below the eye is that it is a stylised snake. The winged eye – a sun disk borne on outstretched wings – occurs commonly among Egyptian tomb inscriptions but was also used by the Assyrians and allied cultures, where the sun disk is sometimes flanked with small snakes.[iii]

The gold mask of Tutankhamun is redolent with symbolic imagery and incorporates aspects of the Wedjat Eye in the eyes of the Pharaoh himself and in the uraeus above the eyes, alongside the head of a vulture. Many photographs of this Pharaoh cut these two figures out of the frame, although they were highly meaningful to the makers of the mask. The vulture goddess was associated with the protection of mothers and children, and of pharaohs. Hence she was the female figure, representing also Upper Egypt, with the cobra representing Lower Egypt as a male figure. The mask has epaulettes of the head of a falcon, and the braided pectoral represents the feathered wings of the goddess Isis. Inscriptions indicate that the right eye represents the sun god, the left eye the moon, the eyebrows the nine gods of creation, the forehead, the jackal-headed god Anubis; and the blue and gold hair, the colours of the sun and the sky, represents Ptah, one of the gods of creation.

The most powerful snake in Egypt was the spitting cobra, and the symbolic representation was the hooded cobra spitting fire. A legend of the earlier third kingdom relates that the god Atum had a sole eye, which, although protective, was liable to be angry and violent. Because of this, Atum changed the eye into a rearing cobra, carrying the Greek name *uraeus*, which ultimately came to guard the crown of the sun god Ra and is part of the forehead crown of the pharaohs, where it has a powerful protective role. However, there is a winged serpent god, Neith, in the Egyptian pantheon, whom the scroll may represent. Finally, the curved eyebrow appears to correspond to the hieroglyph for the arch of the sky, and therefore to the nine gods and goddesses of creation who created it.

In a discussion on illusion and art Gombrich[iv] records that in Sri Lanka, adding eyes to the statue of a Buddha is heavily cloaked in taboo because, by painting them in, the craftsman

Wedjat Eyes from an ancient Egyptian sarcophagus, British Museum

brings the statue to life. He is obliged, like Perseus, to avoid the power of the image he is creating, by looking at the statue through a mirror and painting in the eyes over his shoulder. It is not the eyes themselves, but the meaning that they have, that the person perceives. Coincidentally, this illustrates the original meaning of what the Greeks called *mimesis*, from which we get the words *mimicry* and *imitation*. Aristotle in *The Poetics* used the word to describe what is beyond the 'real' visual image.[v] But during the centuries in which his works survived only in Islamic libraries, the English derivatives that we now use came to refer to processes of copying rather than of interpretation.

The Medusa appears to be a personification of the Evil Eye, the culture of which pervades the folklore of Eastern Europe and parts of Asia. The Eye is a disembodied, unseen spiritual power that brings disease, death or misfortune to those who are unlucky enough to come within its gaze. Myth and superstition surrounding the Eye have survived from prehistory to the present day. They can be traced through the basilisk, which also had a deadly stare, to the eye of the Egyptian sun-god, Horus, and to the use on amulets, charms, clothing, fishing boats, doors and window-frames throughout the Mediterranean and Eastern Europe and East Asia. Images of the eye are intended to repel evil, including the eye itself: seeing an image of itself, especially a reflection in a mirror is lethal to it.

The eye used as an amulet today is usually a bead of blue glass (sometimes white, green and brown, or agate, according to Paine, with a yellow surround outlined in white, and with a black dot in the centre.[vi]

> *"The blue eye bead stares back at the unseen evil eye throughout the Turkic world, from Central Asia to the Middle East and the Mediterranean. Large versions of it hang above doorways in Uzbekistan and at the entrance to the brand-new Hall of Independence in Ashkabad. Babies in Kosovo wear it pinned to their clothes, camels in Jordan and Donkeys in Corfu have it hanging from their harness, roadside stalls in Istanbul sell nothing else."*

Dorothy Carrington[vii] has provided us with a striking account of the Eye that she believes has persisted with little change from prehistoric times to the present in remote villages in the Corsican mountains. Known as *l'occhiu*, the affliction of the Eye shows itself as headaches, nausea, lack of appetite, and physical and mental depression. The Eye may be invisible, associated with

clockwise from top left:
Painted image of a Japanese *hannya* **mask, designed to repel evil spirits**

An modern Evil Eye amulet

An 'eye' ring from the Roman period. Sassari Museum, Sardinia

supernatural beings, witches, or other people who are unaware of possessing it, and is often believed to be a projection of envy, for example from the souls of women who have died in childbirth. It can be dispelled by individuals known as *signatori* who make a diagnosis by floating droplets of oil on water in a plate. If the Eye is there, the effect is transmitted to the *signatora* who becomes ill, but then recovers by breaking the pattern of the oil film and throwing the plate away, casting away the reflection of the Eye also.

The same practice survives also in Sardinia, where it is sometimes used as a form of alternative medicine, particularly for the treatment of skin diseases.[viii] A beautiful gold ring from the Roman period of Sardinia testifies to the antiquity of the Eye in that part of the world.

The handsome Narcissus, who shunned the advances of the beautiful Echo, in spite of the fact that one of her charms was that she would only speak when spoken to first, fell desperately in love with his own reflection. This killed him; he pined away through his inability to possess his own image and provided future generations of psychologists with a role model for a personality disorder. In *The Golden Bough*, Frazer gives many examples from all over the world of the soul being captured by spirits in the reflection from a water surface, or of evil being passed from one being to another. This extends to the belief that a camera captures the soul. I have myself witnessed a sort of panic at the sight of my camera lens in remote tribal villages as far apart as Mexico and Nigeria. In *The Golden Bough*, Frazer relates:

> *"Some villagers in Sikkim betrayed a lively horror and hid away whenever the lens of a camera, or 'the evil eye of the box' as they called it, was turned upon them.... They thought it took away their souls with their pictures and so put it in the power of the owner of the camera to cast spells on them, and they alleged that a photograph of the scenery blighted the landscape."*

A mirror has the same role and function attached to it as a camera lens, so that in many cultures it is believed that the soul is drawn out of the body by the mirror and can escape or be captured by spirits as a result. Alice's passage through the looking glass is an allegory of this: Alice enters the unconscious world of dream images when she passes through the looking glass, and becomes part of the dream herself (and therefore, as Tweedledum and Tweedledee insist, not real at all). So the Evil Eye can destroy itself by projecting its power onto its own image in a mirror, just as the basilisk will die if it sees its own reflection.

Desmond Morris has described the ways in which the fishermen of Malta defend themselves against the Evil Eye.[ix] The boats have a carved wooden eye painted on the prow on each side, which

they believe enables them to counter the Evil Eye by out-staring it. Morris says, "The effect of these eyes was to convert each vessel into a huge piece of surreal, multicoloured sculpture – more of a 'being' than a vessel." Eyes are painted also at the entrance to the Grand Harbour of Malta. Fishing boats with eyes on the prow are found still only in Portugal and the Eastern Mediterranean, and as far east as Bali; the tradition goes back at least to the ancient Romans. The great junks of the Chinese treasure fleets of the fourteenth and fifteenth centuries carried eyes, which were those of dragons.[x]

Images with staring eyes are very common in tribal cultures all over the world, often made more fearsome in a face or mask by the addition of powerful teeth, bat ears, or horns, as in the Indonesian Barong masks, or the Japanese hannya masks. Placed on a wall, these were believed to drive evil spirits away from the house.

E.H. Gombrich in *Art and Illusion* wrote a thought-provoking essay on Pygmalion's Power, in which he examines the desire of the artist to make art come alive. The story of Pygmalion comes from Ovid; he was a sculptor who fell in love with the ivory statue he had created, and asked Venus to provide him with a bride who was like the statue. Venus then made the statue itself come alive. According to Gombrich, this desire to complete the creative process, which an artist is unable to fulfil, was a great frustration for Leonardo da Vinci. It led him to become an engineer, making, among other things, what art historians have called flying machines, but which Leonardo intended to be birds that could fly. He regarded them as his own creations that deserved to be accepted as real birds.

The eye has perhaps the greatest potential to 'give life' to a work of art. The power that eyes gave to Chinese dragons is illustrated by a story going back to the sixth century AD. Zhang Sengyu painted a mural with four dragons, initially without eyes. When he added eyes to two of them there was thunder and lightning, walls cracked and the two-eyed dragons ascended to heaven, while the eyeless ones remained on the wall.[xi]

Skulls recovered from Jericho and dated to 6000 BC had been covered with white plaster to restore the features of the deceased, and the eye sockets contained shells, such as cowries. Similarly, masks and woodcarvings from Indonesia often have cowrie shells for eyes. The effect is striking. Gombrich suggests that this is because we see the shells as in the same 'class' as a true eye: in psychological terms we generalise the image. In other words an eye need not look very much like a living eye to be perceived as such, providing it is set in the right context. This helps us in understanding the diversity of eye-spots on the wings of butterflies and moths. That this also applies to birds has been shown experimentally by David Blest (see page 152).

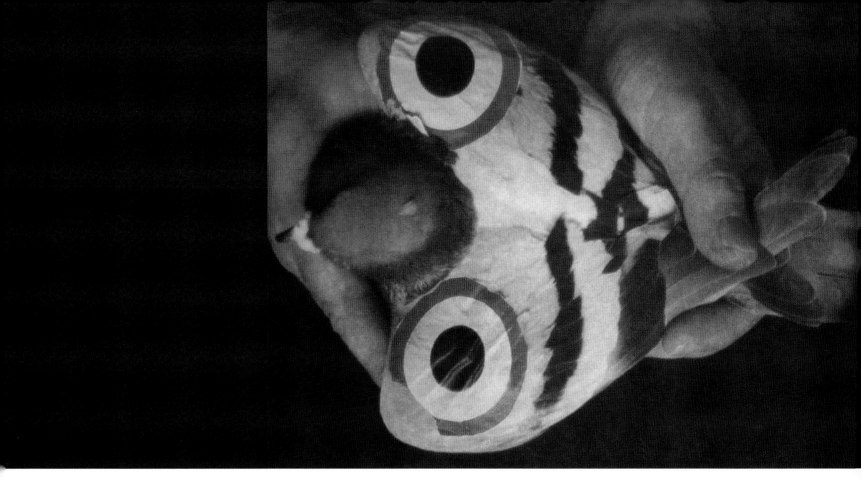

above : **A pigeon receives protection from hawks through the application of large eye-spots to its wings**

opposite left: **A species of the African bush brown butterfly (*Bicyclus*); a butterfly with multiple eye-spots now used in research on inheritance of eye-spots**

opposite right: **Eye-spot balls used commercially as a means of repelling birds from crop fields**

By accentuating the features of the eye, a more powerful image is produced. Outlining the eye with cosmetics is a practice that has been used down the ages by women in order to look more beautiful. Shakespeare says in one of his sonnets

> "*If I could write the beauty of your eyes*
> *And in fresh numbers number all your graces,*
> *The age to come would say, 'This poet lies;*
> *Such heavenly touches ne'er touch'd earthly faces.'*"

In parts of southern India, a preparation known as *kajal*, based on soot from burning sandalwood oil and ghee, is used as an eye cosmetic for women, but is also used to ward off the Evil Eye, when a spot of it is placed at the back of the neck of an infant.

Eye cosmetics were used extensively by the ancient Egyptians from at least 4000 BC. Two colourants were used: green, which was made from malachite (a copper oxide), and black, which was made first from lead sulphide (galena) and then, later, from soot. The green was used in the Old Kingdom and was part of the symbol of the Eye of Horus, which was used in protective amulets. The black pigment from soot is known as 'kohl' in the Arab world and is still used today to make the eyes appear larger and more luminous, to protect the eyelids against the sun, or to counter the Evil Eye.

The white plaster portrait of a woman found in Mycenae represents someone who has made extensive use of cosmetics. White lead (a toxic oxide of lead) was commonly used in ancient times to produce a white face, against which the eyes could be outlined in black. The drawback of this was that the toxin reduced the life expectancy of women to around twenty-five years, and presumably men suffered as well from transfer of the lead. The dominating eyes with dilated pupils have a sense of menace about them, which is reinforced by the fringe on the forehead of snakes' tails, suggesting that the portrait is of a priestess with supernatural powers.

Wooden figurines dating back to 2700-2600 BC found in the temple of Tell Asmar in Sumeria (Iraq) have very large eyes, made from shells and black limestone, which are almost all black because of the expanded pupil. They remain an enigma to archaeologists, most of whom regard them as votives in constant prayer. However, the Wedjat Eye commonly also has a large dilated

black pupil. This form is replicated on ancient Egyptian tombs and sarcophagi and face masks. In the Egyptian section of the British Museum I came across a replica of a sacred bull with the same kind of numinous large circular black pupils – the archetypal bull's eyes that have become the metaphor for the centre. Could it be that the eye of the sacred bull, which is of great antiquity and ubiquity in eastern Mediterranean and Asian cultures, was seen as the black hole forming a conduit to the spiritual world, through which life force and regenerative powers could flow?

We should remember, however, that the sacred owl has large pupils that open wide in the darkness. This is often overlooked because many owl photographs are taken in daylight or with flash, which causes the pupil to contract. The owl eyes are thus still seen in common folklore today as numinous sources of power and perception. There is an echo of this in Milton's poem *Il Penseroso*, as he describes the Goddess Melancholy:

> *… looks commercing with the skies,*
> *Thy rapt soul sitting in thine eyes:*
> *There held in holy passion still,*
> *Forget thyself to marble.*

The German ethologist Irenäus Eibl-Eibesfeldt[xii] made a study of human gestures and facial expressions. His studies were cross-cultural, and he filmed the expressions of people from tribes that had had no previous contact with the western world using a camera that had a smaller lens pointing sideways from the main axis, so that they were unaware they were being filmed. He found that dilation of the pupils was a sign of interest. They was obviously a sign of sexual excitement in a flirting girl from New Guinea whom he filmed.

It is said that businessmen in parts of Asia have always used the unconscious signal of pupil enlargement when negotiating deals: they are able to detect when the price talked about becomes interesting. Certainly, making the pupil larger in the photograph of an attractive woman makes it more appealing to men (and presumably vice versa): a technique used in advertising and promotion. The converse, for example very small pupils in an attractive woman, nullifies her appeal, and has a slightly disturbing effect. The white of the eye is an important social

Paolo Uccello: *St George and the Dragon*

signal, and when it is shown it accentuates the direction of gaze and then signals fear or alarm, especially when associated with a contracted pupil.

It is perhaps worth mentioning that Eibl-Eibesfeldt also showed that the eyebrow amplifies the non-verbal communication of the eyes. The so-called 'eyebrow-flash', in which the eyebrows move up and down rapidly, indicates recognition, and emphasises the desire for eye contact and communication with another individual. Raising of the eyebrows, while it may also indicate surprise, makes the eye appear larger.

E.H. Gombrich noted that any form that resembles a human face immediately grabs our attention. This was put to the test by biologists at Newcastle University.[xiii] The experimenters, Melissa Bateson and her colleagues, found that people were more likely to put money into an honesty box to pay for hot drinks if the box was sited near a poster showing a pair of eyes. They paid between 10p and 30p a litre for milk when pictures of flowers were put above the honesty box, but when the eyes were used the payments shot up to nearly 70p a litre. It appears that this cautious or slightly fearful response to eyes has been important in the evolution of human social behaviour, tending to prevent the development of selfish behaviour. In George Orwell's *Nineteen Eighty-Four* the image of Big Brother is present everywhere. Nowadays, people are not watched by eyes but by cameras, and so have to be reminded continuously that Big Brother is watching them.

Thus the eye has all the attributes of an archetypal image, lighting up our world as does the sun, becoming a source of power like the sun, a means of communicating with the gods, and a protection against evil, which manifests itself through the thousand eyes of the night, whose power is countered only by man-made images.

The ethologist David Blest did a series of experiments[xiv] to determine how insect-eating birds responded to eye-spots, choosing the butterfly *Junonia (Precis) almana* as his model. He did this by training birds to feed on mealworms. He then placed a mealworm equidistant between two artificial eye spots, and found that the birds then tended to avoid the grub, particularly if the eye-spot had a dark centre to it with a white ring outside it. The most effective eye-spot was one composed of non-concentric black rings, which made the image appear three-dimensional, the white ring between two black ones simulating light reflected from the cornea of a real eye.

These experiments confirmed that the birds were responding to a simple sign stimulus, disembodied, as it were, from the owl model. They have also led to practical use for scaring birds. This started with a pigeon fancier in Yorkshire who was becoming increasingly frustrated

as a result of hawks killing his racing pigeons.[xv] He adopted the ruse of painting RAF roundel insignia on the wings of the birds (the roundels, incidentally, are simply another form of the winged eye of ancient civilisations) and found that this protected his birds.

Nowadays, 'eye-spot balls' are coming into use for crop protection. These are formed of large eyes that are usually painted or stuck on to the outside of a balloon, so that the eyes are also seen in movement. Eye-spot balls floated above a crop deter birds from feeding, for at least a period of weeks before the birds discover that the balls are not harmful. Beach balls, which can be floated on the water, are used to deter geese.

The eyes are produced in various combinations of yellow, black and red. And so the Evil Eye is a threat for birds, as it is for humans, but for different reasons. The equivalent for us of a large eye-spot would be the sudden perception of someone aiming a gun in our direction, while a disembodied, staring eye would invoke connected images of power, dread and evil.

The eye-spot as a symbol of terror has also been used in art, notably in Uccello's painting of St George and the Dragon. His fearsome dragon bears some resemblance to *Tyrannosaurus rex*, with its two powerfully-clawed legs, teeth to match, and a serpentine tail. However, this dinosaurian creature has in addition a pair of bat-like wings each with a large eye-spot or roundel, blue with a red rim. The dragon was a representation of the devil in the Middle Ages. St George subdued it with his lance, so that the beautiful princess who was about to be sacrificed was able to lead it tamely away to its final nemesis using her belt as a leash. The roundels actually transform the dragon, drawing the eyes towards the fearsome beast. Roundels with concentric bands of bright colour are used in all kinds of situations in which easy identification is required: they act as beacons for the eye. Hence their use on military aircraft, marking stations on the London Underground, and on heraldic shields. The Spitfire, which has become a symbol of the Battle of Britain in the Second World War, would cease to be awe-inspiring without the large roundels on the wings. This testifies to the archetypal significance of the eye, but we are so used to seeing roundels on military aircraft that the 'eyes' on the wings of Uccello's dragon interfere with the original message of the painting and gives it a surreal air.

Large eye-spots are found in the South American owl butterflies (*Caligo*) and in a few others including the peacock butterfly, but otherwise small eye-spots are common currency amongst butterflies; there are few species that do not have them.

Small eye-spots simulate the eyes of various insectivorous birds, of which there are very many in almost every habitat: tits, flycatchers, jays, thrushes, robins, to mention just a few. It is

often argued that small eye-spots serve as targets for birds to peck at, deflecting attention away from the head and body of the insect, which are the vulnerable parts. The alternative explanation is that, as is the case with large eyes, the insect is presenting the bird or other predator with a puzzle. The questions to be resolved are: 'What does that eye belong to?' 'Is there a body outline to help the interpretation?' It takes time to resolve an ambiguous image because of the need to place the eye in relation to the outline of the figure, so we can assume that it takes time for a bird to resolve a similar puzzle. Only a fraction of a second may be enough time to allow the butterfly or moth to sense the danger and fly off.

There is an additional puzzle that many butterflies pose, and some moths as well. They present a row of small eyes. It may be that this is a means of producing a supernormal stimulus (see Chapter 4) or that the additional puzzle presented is then, 'How many insects are there here?' Small eyes relative to the head are very typical of birds and lizards, among other reptiles, many of which are cryptically coloured and forage on tree-trunks or in rocky areas. It is not therefore surprising to find that many species of butterfly that have cryptic brown or blackish underwings also have small eye-spots. The folded wings then present something like a bird's head in profile, or sometimes as seen from above. Some of the European species of brown butterfly have the colouring and eye of the common robin, while certain butterflies and the silk moth *Antheraea pernyi* have a greater resemblance to lizards. There is also a possibility that rows of small eye-spots in some butterflies simulate the multiple eyes of hunting spiders or the large venomous tropical mygalomorph spiders.

In research designed to test the hypothesis that the role of small eyes is to provide false targets for birds to peck at, Kendra Robertson and Antonio Monteiro experimented with an African butterfly, with the strange Latin name *Bicyclus*.[xvi] It does not look in the least like a bicycle, but is a brown butterfly with a row of small eyespots on the outer edge of the underwings, visible when the wings are closed, as they usually are, and eye-spots on the upper surface of the fore-wings. It turned out that the females paid particular attention to the eye-spots on the upper side of the wings when choosing a mate, so that the males with white ultraviolet-reflecting pupils to

the eye-spot were generally preferred. It could be, then, that in selecting a mate the female is choosing at the same time the most attractive-looking male (to her) and so ensuring that the species has the type of eye-spot that is most effective for defence. In fact, females prefer males with average-sized eye-spots and were not interested in those that had no white pupils, so natural selection is ensuring that the eyes simulate a reflection from the cornea and stay the same size as, perhaps, the birds and lizards that prey on them. The peacock butterfly is one of the most beautiful of British butterflies. I never came across one in the country area in which I grew up, and my first sight of it was a set specimen I ordered from L. Hugh Newman's famous butterfly farm in Kent. Marvelling at its glory in a glass-topped case, it was some time before I realised that the underside was almost completely black, like the surface of bark. This butterfly is long lived, and hibernates in hollow trees and caves, so it needs good protection from predators, which the black colouring affords it during the winter. Its other protection is the ability to make a rustling sound by rubbing together structures in the fore-wings. This sound is rich in ultrasonic frequencies, which protect it from bats in its hibernation quarters. When it is disturbed it flashes open its wings exposing the four huge eye-spots and produces the ultrasonic cries at the same time. It has been shown by experiment that blue tits attack only peacocks that have their eye-spots painted over, and avoid those with untouched eye-spots, especially if they make their rustling sound as well. If the peacocks are captured, the blue tits eat them happily, proving they are not distasteful and the bluff is effective.

The conundrum that is presented by insects such as the peacock, and a number of other butterflies and giant silk moths which have an eye-spot on each wing, can be understood by the 'double vision' illusion. The British government brought out a poster supporting the "Don't drink and drive" campaign in which a girl's face is portrayed as it would appear if you were seeing double. The result is a highly disturbing image which the mind seeks to resolve but cannot. We search for the ambiguity, but there is none: that is the illusion. Whether other vertebrates are similarly nonplussed by four eyes is of course an open question, but my guess is that primate insectivores, at least, would be.

Bird
Icons

*"He thought he saw an Albatross
That fluttered round the lamp:
He looked again, and found it was
A Penny-Postage-Stamp."*

Lewis Carroll: *Sylvie and Bruno*

I f the poisons in a butterfly killed the birds that tried to eat it, the memory of that experience would obviously be lost. That kind of situation has prompted most biologists to ignore the possibility that insects might evolve into mimics of deadly creatures. But this is wrong: many dangerous animals have startling threat displays, and we have seen that in primates, at least, there is an innate propensity to learn rapidly to distrust snakes. However, much of this is beside the point if we accept that ambiguity and illusion provide an effective defence by briefly disrupting perception: then it does not matter whether the ambiguity involves an image of a deadly animal or not, only whether that image is easily recognisable. It should be added that insectivorous birds and lizards move extremely rapidly when they are foraging: a bird will often search a bush in just a few seconds, skimming through the branches. The decision about whether to pass something by as possibly inedible must therefore be made within a few milliseconds, allowing no time for closer inspection.

We can be reasonably certain that the image an animal recognises most easily is one of its own kind. We know this from the studies that have been done on the phenomenon of imprinting. Konrad Lorenz captured everyone's attention and wonder when he described the way in which young ducklings he had reared by hand followed him around as they would have followed their own natural parent. In this process they maintained a constant distance from him, which was dictated by the angle subtended by his upright figure. The consequence of this was that if he went swimming with them they got closer and closer until they climbed on his head as he started to submerge. In the absence of a parent figure, goslings that were allowed to see only a wooden box for a period after hatching even imprinted upon that and would follow it when it was moved around. This remarkable attachment process, which is found in some form in most vertebrate animals, depends upon the young learning as quickly as possible what they can see, hear and smell. That is, they learn what is safe and constant in their environment. Until they are fully aware of that, they cannot distinguish the unusual from the usual, and the unfamiliar may be a predator or some other threatening circumstance.

Obviously, although an animal may not have a sense of self, it must be able to recognise its own kind. Until it can do that, a predator cannot learn which animals can be killed as prey.

So we may expect to find that butterflies and moths, among other insects, carry iconic representations of their principal predators, so that what is suggested to a predator is the presence of one of its own kind. We might also expect that these iconic designs are generally lacking in precise detail, because that would increase the ambiguity and confuse the predator. However, it may be an illusion of ours that detail often appears to be lacking. Perhaps birds and reptiles are able to see colours and pick out features that we cannot: we need to pause to consider this.

Hermann von Helmholtz, who was famous for his studies of the human eye, would have been more impressed with the eye of a bird. Birds have the most highly developed eyes in the animal kingdom: they have the super deluxe version compared with us. While the human eye accounts for one per cent by weight of the head, in most birds it is fifteen per cent, and in owls the eyes weigh more than the brain. A sparrow has about twice as many light-sensitive cells in the retina as a human, and hawks have five times as many. In the fovea, which is the central area of the retina upon which the lens focuses light, hawks and falcons have four to eight times as many cones (colour sensitive cells) per square millimetre as humans, giving them a correspondingly greater resolution of distant objects. To put this in perspective, when compared with the average digital camera, which has a five megapixel image spread over the area of the screen, a hawk would have the equivalent of over five thousand megapixels in just one square millimetre of the central fovea, which is the most sensitive area of the retina.

It has been discovered recently that many birds are *quadrichromatic*;[i] that is, they have four types of cone cell. To get an idea of what this means, try adjusting the colour control on your television or computer so that the yellow or green is turned right down: then you realise the value of being able to see three primary colours. Now the other refinement of bird vision is the tuning of the sensitivity of the cones of the bird eye to different wavelengths of light from the cones of the human eye. It is impossible for us to imagine the consequences of this. We see blue at a wavelength of around 437 lamda, green at 533, and red at 564. We have no idea about how birds see colours, but the wavelengths at which their cones are sensitive are 362, 449, 504 and 563 (this varies between species): a quick glance suggests that red may be detected equally well, but then their spectral chart must be entirely different, and it seems that they will see more

top: **Male of Rajah Brooke's birdwing butterfly (*Trogonoptera brookiana*). A.R. Wallace saw immediately the images of the tips of green covert feathers, which show as if proceeding out of the shade of forest vegetation**

above: **A set specimen of Rajah Brooke's birdwing. The illusion of green feather tips on the wings is not easily seen in this position because of the unnatural wing orientation**

above left: **The Australian
blue mountain swallowtail
(*Papilio ulysses*)**

above right: ***P. ulysses* with
the wings slightly folded,
accentuating the bird-like
wings and feathers**

colours than we do. This supposition is confirmed by experiments in which pigeons were trained by conditioning them to peck at a disk in response to colour signals. The results showed that they discriminated much better than we do between different wavelengths of light, so they could see a much greater range of hues, inviting a comparison with the way in which we discriminate slight differences of wavelength of sound as in a chromatic scale. Birds may have something like a twelve-note scale of colour while we have about half that, corresponding roughly to red, blue, green, yellow, and violet.

The presence of extra types of colour receptor in the bird eye mean that, in addition to ultraviolet, birds can see colours that are hidden to us. The common test for colour blindness involves a matrix of colour spots, some of which are a different colour from the background and are visible as a number, like two or eight. If the number spots contain red pigment and the rest are green, a red-green colour-blind person will not see the number. So we do not know what patterns and designs a bird may see on a butterfly's wing because we are colour blind relative to a bird. We cannot find this out by scanning a photograph because a standard colour photograph is taken with a trichromatic film.

The four-cone system, then, with sensitivity in the ultraviolet (which is not a colour to us, although we can detect the brightness of reflected ultraviolet light from water or the clouds when we remove our sun-glasses) enables birds to see features that we are unaware of. For example, kestrels, while hovering, can detect the presence of voles by the ultraviolet light reflected from their scent marks on the vegetation.[ii] Blue tits are attracted to potential mates by the high UV reflection from parts of their blue plumage, and they can also detect cryptically coloured

caterpillars of the winter moth and cabbage moth by the slightly higher amount of UV reflected from them than from the vegetation.[iii]

It has even been suggested that the magnetic sense of migratory birds projects patterns onto their visual field; that is, that they may be aware of some visual pattern which changes as they change direction with respect to the Earth's magnetic field.

It is well known that many of the white and sulphur butterflies that appear to us to have no patterning on their wings, do in fact have patterns that can be captured on UV-sensitive film. The insects themselves make use of this in communicating with each other: UV patterns representative of the species and of the sex are commonly found on the wings of yellow and white butterflies. This allows them to broadcast signals in a visual channel that is not available to some of their predators – primates for example.

The main predators of butterflies and moths are, of course, birds, and the images that signify a bird are the beak, head and eyes, feathers, tail fan, and barring on the plumage. Such icons are found in profusion among butterflies and moths, but are "not known, because not looked for."[iv] A marvellous example of the use of feather images to suggest the presence of a bird is found in one of the most strikingly beautiful of all butterflies, known as Rajah Brooke's birdwing (*Trogonoptera brookiana*). It was given this name by Alfred Russel Wallace, who in his epic journey around the islands of what was then known as the Malay Archipelago (and now comprises Indonesia, Malaysia and Papua New Guinea) came across this insect in 1856 in Sarawak, where the Englishman Sir James Brooke, known as Rajah Brooke, was the regional governor. Wallace described it in his book *The Malay Archipelago* thus:

The African migrant butterfly (*Catopsilia florella*) showing wing patterns revealed under near-ultraviolet light, visible to birds and butterflies but not to humans

The birdwing butterflies are aptly named, not only for the size of their wings, but also for the shape. The fore-wings are usually much larger than the hindwings, with a curved leading edge. Rajah Brooke's birdwing in its natural pose is large enough to be mistaken for a small bird and the iridescent green wing-tips, as if projecting from the dark shade so that they catch the sunlight, allow the eye to extrapolate an image of the whole bird on that dark background. When we see live butterflies, the wings are inclined, partially folded, moved in certain axes and displaced one against the other, so that certain features stand out and suddenly become apparent. But when we look at a set specimen of Rajah Brooke's birdwing, the illusion of the tips of covert feathers on opened wings is lost.

Wallace's hitherto neglected suggestion of bird-mimicry suggests that there might be feather patterns on other large butterflies, and you do not have to search very far to find them. Other birdwings and many swallowtails have feathery images painted by Nature on their fore-wings. The beautiful blue mountain swallowtail, for example, has iridescent blue feather markings on its wings, which become particularly visible when the fore-wings are slightly retracted.

The excitement of every naturalist and scientist who makes a genuine discovery, often for the first time in man's history, is imbued in Wallace's famous description of his capture of a new species of birdwing near Ternate in the Moluccas (by coincidence the place from which he wrote his letter to Darwin setting out the principle of evolution by natural selection).

above left: **Photomicrograph of the wing scales of a morpho butterfly. Each scale is a multilayered structure and the iridescence is generated by interference of light rays reflected from the various layers**

"The beauty and brilliance of this insect are indescribable, and none but a naturalist can understand the intense excitement I experienced when I at length captured it. On taking it out of my net and opening the glorious wings, my heart began to beat violently, the blood rushed to my head, and I felt much more like fainting than I have done when in apprehension of immediate death. I had a headache the rest of the day, so great was the excitement produced by what will appear to most people a very inadequate cause."

above right: **A male morpho butterfly (*Morpho peleides*)**

This prompts one to wonder whether brilliant colours *per se* can have a shock effect on predators searching for insects that are normally concealed or camouflaged by their colours, even when such bright colours are not part of a startle display that involves a sudden change of form and aspect.

The morpho butterflies of South American forests provide a good illustration: their undersides are dull brown in colour, but when they fly through the forest the iridescent upper surfaces flash bright in the sunlight and they can be seen from low-flying aircraft. Henry Walter Bates,[v] writing about *Morpho rhetenor* in the Amazon forest, called it quite a dazzling lustre, adding, "When it comes sailing along, it occasionally flaps its wings, and then the blue surface flashes in the sunlight so that it is visible a quarter of a mile off." The American naturalist William Beebe described a morpho butterfly thus: "When, in flight, the fore-wings were suddenly spread and raised, the effect in sunlight was of an electric light suddenly flashed into one's eyes. The result gave a good chance of escape, whether from lizard, monkey, bird, or man."[vi] Scientists at Exeter University have found that up to 75 per cent of the incident blue light falling on the wings of *Morpho rhetenor*, including ultraviolet light, is reflected back to produce the dazzling blue colour, which arises from interference of light rays refracted through crystal-like scales with built-in diffraction gratings.[vii] This is a remarkably high level of reflectance, which is greater than can be achieved from a pigmented surface without such diffraction mechanisms and can be compared to reflection of about 90 per cent of light from an ordinary silvered mirror, or from snow, which in the case of reflected sunlight is sufficient to damage the eyes if the sun is viewed directly.

It would be wrong to assume that such bright colours exist solely for the purpose of distracting predators: indeed, we can only speculate about this. It is only the male morphos that dazzle, the females are usually dull coloured, suggesting that the iridescence has much to do with courtship behaviour, as Darwin believed, and maintenance of territory among males. Members of one tribe on the Rio Negro attract male *Morpho rhetenor* with blue lures and then use the wings in tribal costumes. However, UV reflectance may be hidden from us by brown scales in the females.

We should also take into account that the plumage of many tropical birds is iridescent, and it may be that butterflies benefit by having iridescent colours on their wings – something that is achieved by a special microstructure of the scales so that they act as diffraction gratings.

above left: **An example of the use of set butterflies (here *Morpho rhetenor*) as a symbol of natural purity. Part of an advertisement for Clipper coffee**

above right: **The purple emperor butterfly (*Apatura iris*). The head of a bird can be detected at the end of each hind-wing**

above left: **The swallowtail**
(*Papilio polymnestor*), which
has features of a bird: the wide
curved blackish fore-wings
with white feather tips on the
posterior edges, and hind-wings
marked like a tail fan with black
distal markings heightening the
impression of white feather tips

above right: **The swallowtail**
(*Papilio rumanzovia*), which has
feather markings and red patches
similar to bird wing flashes, and
also has a white band on the
hind-wings similar to that on the
tail fan of swallows

opposite: **The European scarce**
swallowtail (*Iphiclides podalirius*
***feisthamelii*) seen from an angle**
that suggests a bird's head and
beak, perhaps as a bird
might often see it

So iridescence is frequently associated with eye-spots, feather markings, and even portrayal of beaks. The purple emperor butterfly is a beautiful example: its hindwings have readily discernable eyes and beaks, each hind-wing sporting a bird's head.

There were many days in my career when I had to endure what was, for me, the inexorable boredom of committee meetings, which I tried to counter by doodling on my agenda sheet. My favourite doodle was a butterfly, usually a peacock, with a large eye-spot on each wing. Whatever this said about my unconscious desires to fly out of the window on silent wings on such occasions – and about other proclivities I must be unaware of – the fact remained that the butterfly I drew would have been incapable of flying properly because its wings were splayed out in the 'set' position. The study of butterfly evolution and classification has always been based upon specimens that have been killed, pinned and 'set' in the conventional way that displays the whole of the surface of the wings, opened horizontally. This involves fixing the wings in positions that they never assume in life, and allowing them to harden in that position with the forewings pulled forwards so that their posterior borders lie along a straight line. The insect in a cabinet is always viewed with the body axis in line with the eye.

A butterfly is never seen in this set position when alive, although this is the kind of image we are most familiar with and readily accept in art, advertising and product branding. Such images are commonly used, incongruously, to epitomise what is natural (and by implication pure and healthy). Very importantly for the issues that we are considering now, in the set position the patterns and designs that regale the wings of all butterflies and moths are disrupted: you no longer see all that is there in the living insect. Setting a butterfly is a bit like unfolding origami.

Nonetheless, butterfly symbols used in design and ornamentation almost always appear this way. The coffee cup I am drinking from as I write has blue butterflies on it that are quite unnatural to me, but which presumably would not be considered a sufficiently eye-catching design for a marketable product if they were portrayed in a natural pose, so much has our perception been fashioned by repeated exposure to printed images. Convention in design occurs without us realising it: the butterflies in the paintings of the Dutch and Flemish Old Masters look a little strange to us today. Although they were meticulously observed, twentieth century artists portrayed them differently. Illustrators of natural history books will sometimes even take a pinned butterfly and put it onto foliage in the apparent belief that it will be seen as 'natural'.

Many artists too, including Salvador Dalí, portray set butterflies. One of Dalí's pictures is an anamorphic construction based on arrangements of set butterflies that transmute into a figure of Don Quixote when reflected on the surface of a cylindrical mirror. His work *Mad Mad Mad Minerva* uses a set nymphalid butterfly to represent the soul of Minerva.

Swallows and martins are common insect feeders that have a worldwide distribution, excluding only the polar regions and most of Australasia. The sobriquet to the swallowtail family of butterflies indicates a perceived mimesis, even though few people would take seriously the suggestion that the resemblance of the butterflies to swallows is more than an evolutionary coincidence.

Let us now examine this assumption in more detail. If we start by looking at the features used in bird identification handbooks we find the following:

Silhouettes in flight
Tail plumage
Form of the bill
Wing patches – flashes of conspicuous vivid colour on the wings
Wing stripes – bands of bright contrasting colour (e.g. yellow or white)
White or coloured bars on the wings or body
Type of movement
Relative size of the eyes.

It appears that evolution has equipped birds and other predators with a similar mental identification guide so that they are able to recognise other birds and other animals present in the same environment on the basis of certain key features. Careful examination shows that swallowtail and birdwing butterflies have evolved wing patterns and other features that replicate these key features. Although they may not fool an ornithologist using an identification guide, they will momentarily raise questions marks in the minds of birds and other predators about the nature of the creature they have encountered.

Two swallowtails (*Papilio machaon*). Rotate this page through 90° and then 180°

The silhouette with curved fore-wings overshadowing the hind-wings is much more birdlike than that of butterflies of other families, and white feather-markings are found on the fore-wings of some species, such as *Papilio polymnestor*. This is a species of the swallowtail family without the typical swallow's tail, in which the hind-wings are marked, sometimes with a scalloped pattern, simulating a tail fan. In species with long tails these can be construed as the forked tail of swallows or martins, and the affinity is reinforced by the typical hovering flight of the insects while feeding, when the wings are in constant motion, as the wings of a bird would have to be when hovering.

The function of the long tails in the giant lunar or moon moths may also be to simulate birds of the swallow family. The Indian moon moth, *Actias selene*, flies at dusk when it forms a dark image against the sky, and the flight has been described by one observer[viii] thus, "Males in flight provide a perfectly magnificent spectacle; their movement is of astonishing swiftness and agility, not, in fact, unlike that of a house martin."

The house martin and the swallow have red patches behind the eyes, and a large white band at the base of the tail fan, features that can be detected in a variety of swallowtail species from

above: **The sword-tail butterfly (*Pathysa antiphates*). A butterfly with bird beaks formed by the tail**

below: **The dragon-tail (*Lamproptera curius*). While the tails resemble an open beak the insect also looks like a dragonfly when in flight**

South-East Asia. Wing patches or stripes of bright colour combined with white bands on the hind-wings are commonly found in swallowtails, as they are in birds, *Papilio rumanzovia* being an example. This is a Batesian mimic of *Papilio aristolochiae*, the caterpillars of which tolerate the poisons that accumulate in their bodies and feed on poisonous Aristolochia vines, whose bright markings serve as a warning of their toxic nature.

The majority of swallowtails have tails that can also be construed as simulacra of a bird's beak. This impression is heightened by the presence of an eye-spot at the base of each hind-wing, so that when the insect is seen hovering while feeding, or from the side at rest, there is an indistinct image of a bird's head with an open beak. A good example is the common European tiger swallowtail (known as the scarce swallowtail in Britain, because that is what it is). In the set position the two tails are set well apart and each has a small eye-spot at the base. This has often led to the suggestion that the false eyes are targets for insectivorous birds, directing attack away from the head of the butterfly. However, when the butterfly is hovering over a flower, the two tails are brought together, and when viewed from the side the image is of an open beak with the eye at the base in a black patch, just as in many birds. At first glance you may not be convinced, but you need to adjust your mind to two things. First, as we

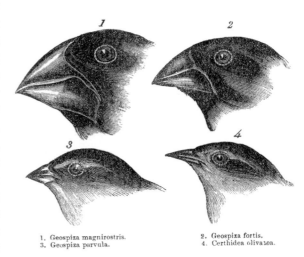

1. Geospiza magnirostris.
2. Geospiza fortis.
3. Geospiza parvula.
4. Certhidea olivasea.

have seen, animals do not have Gestalt perception but see the detail first, so if we detach the tail end from an image then the small picture we see is unencumbered by all the other aspects of the big picture that influence our perception and are telling us this is the tail of a butterfly. Secondly, the current view is that man developed an upright gait at a very early stage in evolution and did not evolve from an ancestor like modern apes, which use all fours. Hence because we tend to keep our bodies upright all the time and the familiar things in our environment – other people, trees, buildings, etc. – are nearly always seen in the vertical plane, we have difficulty recognising a bird or any other object if it is not 'the right way up'. There are a number of visual illusions that show this effect, which is based on expectation.[ix]

Try this simple experiment with the illustration on page 166, which shows two swallowtail butterflies feeding on thistles. If you rotate the illustration 90° clockwise, one swallowtail will become bird-like, with an eye, open beak, and barred tail feather. Rotate through 180° and the other swallowtail becomes a strange creature with sickle-shaped jaws. Notice also that the eye-spots encapsulate the colour pattern on the head of a swallow: blue, red and white, which may be far more distracting to another bird than it is to us.

Most insectivorous birds forage in trees and bushes for insects, and need to be able to identify them from any position in space. It is tempting to infer that there can be no 'right way up' for them as there is for us. Watch a bird foraging in a shrubbery. Whatever the orientation of its body in space (and this goes as well for farmyard hens and pheasants that forage on the ground) the head moves in jerks on the body. The bird, to compensate for its lack of binocular vision, is taking a series of rapid snapshots from different viewpoints to gather information about the distance of objects. It can only focus on an object like an insect with one eye, so it is effectively putting that eye in two separate places and gaining information about the distance of the object, much as a surveyor does with a theodolite.

above left: **The pearl-bordered fritillary (*Boloria euphrosyne*)**

above right: **A male European kestrel (*Falco tinnunculus*) with fritillary-patterned wing feathers**

At the same time, the bird gets more information about the shape and size of the object from parallax and the changes in perspective.

Amazing likenesses to birds are also seen in the sword-tail butterfly, *Pathysa antiphates*, and the dragon-tail butterfly *Lamproptera curius*, two insects in which what we see as tails could be ambiguous features, equally well interpreted as an open beak from some perspectives. The dragon-tail is also a dragonfly mimic, beating its largely transparent fore-wings very rapidly and continuously. In this case the long tails imitate the body of the dragonfly.

Momentarily, then, a bird with a long sharp beak focussing on a swallowtail butterfly may perceive the image of a similar bird as if 'through a glass darkly', and hesitate briefly. As might be expected from my hypothesis, different types of beak can be found corresponding to the species of bird found in different habitats.

The beak image is almost always associated with an eye-spot, which provides the vital context for recognition of the beak and its orientation. Beak simulacra are found in butterflies with small eye-spots at the apices of the fore-wings, including many of the brown butterflies. When a butterfly is disturbed it immediately closes its wings, which makes it virtually invisible in the body axis, but it remains much more apparent viewed from the side. Now we find that the underside of the hind-wing of many satyrid (brown) butterflies is cryptically coloured, and when the fore-wings are concealed by them the insect blends in with its surroundings. The underside of the fore-wing, however, typically carries an eye-spot on a coloured brownish background. When the fore-wing is lifted slightly above the hind-wing when the butterfly is at rest with its wings folded, the outer edge defines a short beak below the eye spot. This then resembles the beak of a passerine bird, such as a sparrow.

One of the most enduring memories of my childhood was of red admiral butterflies feeding on the juice of fallen pears beneath our huge pear tree. While taking photographs for this book, I began to wonder again for what rhyme or reason the intricate designs on the underside of the closed wings had evolved. I studied my photographs for hours one day and then I saw a painted blue eye ring and then a triangular beak, and suddenly the head of a goldfinch was in front of me with the characteristic black red and yellow bands. At that point I nearly fell off my chair. In former times, before the industrial revolution, goldfinches were to be found in huge numbers, and were trapped for food. They are found wherever there are thistles and teazles, on the same kind of open land where nettles abound, which are the food plant of the red admiral caterpillars. The image is visible only from certain angles, and is slightly anamorphic. One can imagine the effect on a bird

foraging among the leaves when a resting butterfly raises its fore-wings above the bark-like closed hind-wings and the features of a goldfinch suddenly appear like a conjuror's rabbit out of hat. It requires concentration for us to see an image like this, because the perception of a butterfly dominates, but this is not likely to be so for a bird, as I have already argued.

Mimicry of the beaks of birds such as finches is commonly found in some of the giant silk moths. As typical moths, their wings fold horizontally and the upper surfaces are normally all that is visible to a predator. In some species, an eye-spot on the upper surface of the fore-wing represents a bird's eye, and a line across the wing represents the base of the beak, so that the beak ends in a point at the junction with the body. The head and beak patterns on the fore-wings become very evident if you

focus on just one wing, as in the *Polythysana* moth on page 168. Then, the resemblance to a finch is very clear. *Polythysana* is an astonishing illusionist. Each fore-wing can be conceived equally as a tapir head, with the tip of the snout at the wing-tip and the white-fringed lips below. Invert the page and the eyes and snout of a rodent head appear.

The plumage of birds often has barred patterns. This is distinctive, for example, in many hawk and owl species, where the feathers on the breast and underside of the wings, and often the tail feathers as well, have black bars on a pale background. I have already mentioned that small birds respond to barring when they are mobbing owls. Barred patterns are common in butterflies, but to our eyes they are details that you see only if you look for them. They occur on the wings of fritillary butterflies, on the fore-wings of some swallowtails, and on some nymphalid butterflies such as tortoiseshells and pansy butterflies.

No explanation has hitherto been found for the prevalence of the black-flecked orange wings that are common to fritillary butterflies and are also found in the comma butterfly (*Polygonia c-album*) and a number of other European species. This puzzle is solved convincingly when we turn to the most common predator on small birds in Europe – the common kestrel. This bird, which was much more abundant in earlier times than it is now, overlaps in distribution with almost all the fritillary species and has plumage that is strikingly similar to the fritillary wing pattern.

The tortoiseshell butterflies have barred feather markings along the edge of the fore-wings, which in the small tortoiseshell might equally be said to represent wasp markings, and the same is true of the European swallowtail (*Papilio machaon*). Many swallowtails and some of the pansy butterflies (*Junonia* and *Precis* spp.) have both eye-spots and barred feather marks. The interesting point here is that none of these features is configured on the wings to give a representation of a whole bird, but are isolated signs on the wings, conforming to the idea I presented in earlier chapters that animals react principally to abstracted features of another animal – the 'sign stimuli' of the ethologists.

The peacock pansy butterfly has two sets of eyes of different sizes, and feather markings on the leading edges of the fore-wings, which are all identifiers of birds for another animal but which do not suggest a bird to us because they are in a haphazard configuration. In addition, the eyes on the hind-wings of this butterfly are unlike normal eye-spots with a central black pupil, but have two white 'teeth' in the centre. The eye-spot can thus be construed as a small, open-mouthed snake.

Butterflies are particularly vulnerable to predation when they are mating, and while *in copula* they can have an appearance that is very surreal, which possibly gives them greater protection than they have individually. Mating swallowtails resemble birds with open wings that have barred plumage.

We must be careful not to forget that many factors can influence the colours on the wings of butterflies, including the need for colour displays in courtship, concealment, and regulation

of body temperature. Butterflies function only when their body temperatures have reached a minimum, and before they become active they often have to sun themselves to raise the body temperature, which means exposing the wings more or less horizontally to intercept as much of the sun's rays as possible. The need for thermoregulation therefore influences colour patterns. Colours that absorb the lower wavelengths of light – orange, red and black – are very commonly found on the upper surfaces, especially of butterflies from cooler temperate regions. The wings act as miniature solar panels to gather heat, which is then transmitted to the body through the blood circulating in the wing veins. The body itself tends to be black as well (for example in the tortoiseshell butterfly) so that it absorbs the sun's heat. One consequence of the need to absorb heat is that butterflies need to spend some time basking with the wings open to the sun's rays, but they are better protected from predators when the wings are folded over their backs, when symmetry cues, by which a predator can more easily identify an insect, are suppressed.

Moths, on the other hand, are able to raise their body temperatures by exercising their wing muscles without actually beating the wings – a bit like shivering – to gain heat, and in night-flying moths displays of coloured wings are not generally used in courtship. They rely instead on chemical communication, using scents (pheromones) that are attractive or stimulating to the opposite sex. We therefore find that many moth species show a resemblance to animals that forage at night, pre-eminent among which are owls and smaller primates such as tarsiers, lemurs and tamarins, marmosets and other primates with the common features of large staring eyes.

Two mating swallowtail butterflies (*Eurytides marcellus*). The resemblance to a bird unfolding its wings is obvious

Goddesses

"…In all manifestations of goddesses and gods as animals, birds,
reptiles and insects, … precise and practical reverence for the sacred
drama of nature must be remembered."

Anne Baring & Jules Cashford[i]: *The Myth of the Goddess*

"Where are you going, where are you going?
 To where the wonderful feather plumes lie,
To the field of battle, to the place of the gods:
There, where our mother Itzpapalotl,
moth of obsidian
prepares for the battle in red and yellow."

Cantos Mexicanos de Tenochtitlan, transl. from Grabey[ii]

T he owl is a connecting thread running through this narrative, one with which we began, and one which permeates the spiritual life of man from the earliest periods of civilisation. The gallery of owls in the Tuc d'Audoubert cave in southern France, for example, dates back to 14-16 000 BC. No doubt even in those distant epochs birds represented mastery of the air and ascendance to the afterlife, and their eyes have always had a numinous quality.

The eyes of birds cannot move in their sockets, like ours, and an owl has binocular vision over only 60°-70°, so it has to turn its head directly towards you in order to see you. It can do this with great speed, the head swivelling up to 270° on the neck vertebrae. This means we are not likely to see a live owl in profile, although most other birds, including hawks, which look at you with one eye, are usually photographed or shown in illustrations from the side view. The prehistoric cave owls are therefore easily identified by the rounded head and the forward facing eyes, and are very similar to the owl deities of the ancient Maya on the other side of the Atlantic. It is just these features that are closest to those of a human face and often leave archaeologists in some doubt about how to interpret them. It is not surprising that in earlier times man has incorporated owls into his religious mythology, and that owls to the present day are regarded as 'wise' (like Owl in A.A. Milne's Winnie the Pooh, who was the ultimate authority despite his dreadful spelling). Hegel made the famous comment "the owl of Minerva flies only at dusk" implying that wisdom accrues only in man's later years.

The tombs of Los Millares in Almeria (south-eastern Spain) are curiously eye-shaped, consisting of several concentric rings of stones with the burial chamber in the 'pupil'. These date from 4000 to 3000 BC. They contain striking red bowls and jars with eye-spot designs on them, known as *oculi*. Marija Gimbutas[iii] interprets these as the numinous regenerating eyes of the owl goddess. Menhirs with such oculi that are half owl and half woman have been found from the same period in many places in Europe, including Portugal, Spain, Ireland, southern France and Brittany.

Sculptures or pottery representing an owl goddess have been found in the settlement of Çatal Hüyük in present-day Turkey and in Sumeria (which was once part of modern-day Iraq). Anne

previous page: **Wing-tips of the Ceanothus moth (*Hyalophora euryalus*)**

above: **Ceanothus moth (*Hyalophora euryalus*). Various images can be construed from the design at the edge of the wings: a) a caiman, with the eye at the apex of the fore-wing and the jaws projecting backwards b) a snake's head turned towards the observer at the wing-tip with its body traced along the edges of the fore- and hind-wings c) a millipede with its head at the wing-tip**

Baring and Jules Cashford[iv] have traced the owl symbol back to the Neolithic period, and show that the owl was part of a complex trinity including the bull and the moon, which were symbols of regeneration. This persisted to the times of the Sumerians, whose principal deity Inanna derived her name from that of the owl. Inanna descended into the underworld and was killed by what probably became known as the Evil Eye, and was then resurrected. In her owl form, she represented the world beyond death (because of the association of owls with the night, we presume), and this connection was carried on to the Greeks and Romans and has persisted to some extent to the present day.

According to Pliny, the ancient Greeks and Romans regarded the owl as a bird of ill omen, and when one appeared on the Capitol in Rome it caused such a panic that the building had to be 'disinfected' with sulphur and water to get rid of any evil it may have brought. This association of owls with death and often evil appears widespread in different parts of the world, but owls were also used to repel evil influences. This may explain the significance of adornments to temples and burial chambers.

One of the curious things about the spiritual beliefs of the ancient Egyptians is the almost complete absence of the butterfly as a symbol of the soul. Its place is pre-empted somewhat by the scarab beetle, which is a symbol of death and regeneration, and by the god Horus, with the head and wings of a falcon. The Egyptian mythology, though, included an owl-like bird called the Ba bird, again confusing man and owl, with a face like a human on the body of an owl; it accompanied the soul on its journey to the afterlife.

In European folklore the owl (like the death's head hawk moth) has been associated with the approach of death. Apart from being creatures of the night that fly on silent wings (the feathers are modified to reduce noise, which would alert their prey), their cries have an other world tonality. Shakespeare frequently referred to owls as harbingers of death or other misfortune.

Birds of many species react strongly to owls, as they do also to hawks and eagles. A perched owl, or even a wooden model of an owl, attracts small birds, which mob it furiously in attempts to drive it away. Mobbing involves special calls that alert and attract other birds; a bird giving these

above left: **Ringed eyes from a Minoan sarcophagus from Armeno (Crete), possibly representing the regenerating eye of a goddess, replicated in a deer, or providing protection against evil spirits. Rethymnon Museum, Crete**

top right: **Owl figures engraved in the rock of the 'Owl Gallery' of the Tuc d'Audoubert cave (11-14 000 BC)**

bottom right: **Oculi representing owl eyes on a pot from Sardinia (Ozieri period, c. 4000-3200 BC). Museu Sanna, Sassari**

calls attracts not only more of its own species, but other birds as well. A mixed flock soon gathers with birds swooping down and making mock attacks on the owl.

The so-called 'owl butterflies' of the neotropics (*Caligo* spp.) are generally held to be striking examples of owl mimics, but that assumption has little basis. The males commonly have iridescent blue patches on the upper side of their wings, but the two hind underwings each carry a very prominent eye-spot.

These butterflies are usually photographed in the set position from underneath, head downwards, when there is a very strong resemblance to an owl's head. The difficulty, though, is that in nature these insects never stand on their heads and spread their wings out with the undersides uppermost. Instead they clap their wings tight together above their bodies so there is no chance of a view of a fake owl's head. If we take another look at the underwing, what stands out is the large eye set into a dark area, which approximates the shape of an amphibian head, and at the base of this is a circular area which is positioned where the tympanum (ear-drum) of a frog or toad would be. Many frogs and toads have a flag-shaped dark patch around the eye, and this in fact matches very closely with the wing marking. One species that illustrates this point is the South American cane toad, *Bufo marinus*, which is now fairly widespread throughout the world, but the same image also occurs in some other toads and in some tree frogs. So, once you shake off your heavily prejudiced interpretation of Caligo being an owl mimic, the wing becomes the head of a toad against a piece of bark, if only for a brief moment, and the insect should in my opinion be known by the less romantic name of 'toad butterfly'.

If my supposition is correct, then it is surely no coincidence that toads produce some of the most powerful toxins of all animals, known as 'bufotoxins', which are secreted mainly from glands in the skin. They are produced by the notorious cane toad, among others, and in small doses produce violent hallucinations which can lead people to irrational behaviour. Larger doses affect the heart and respiratory system and block the uptake of oxygen in the blood, often proving fatal. It is said that a Colombian tribe has used the toxins in place of curare in poison arrows.

Certain giant silk moths, in contrast with the Caligos, are without doubt modelled on the faces of owls, and others upon those of small primates. Experiments with models have shown that the eyes of the owl are the most threatening features to other birds.[v] Robert Hinde found that the aspects of a model most likely to provoke mobbing by chaffinches were the general outline with a large head and a short tail, brown and grey coloration, spots, streaks and bar

opposite: **An owl butterfly (*Caligo memnon*) in which the under-wing is adorned with an image resembling the head of a frog or lizard (seen more clearly in the re-orientated enlargement)**

above: **The poisonous cane toad (*Bufo marinus*), one of several probable true models for the 'owl butterfly'. The tympanum is clearly visible behind the eye**

patterns, and forward facing eyes with a beak. These features are all to be found among moths of the family Saturniidae (the giant silk moths). Many of these moths have cryptically patterned fore-wings resembling dead leaves or bark, have strongly marked eyes on the hind-wings and none on the fore-wings. When the moth is at rest the hind-wings are concealed. When disturbed, such a moth will rear up and flash open its hind-wings. The eyes are similar to the eyes of owls and insectivorous primates (monkeys, bush-babies, tarsiers, tamarins, etc.), and in some species, when the insect is viewed in a head downwards position, the illusion of the face of an owl is intensified by the hind-wings parting slightly to expose the abdomen, which then resembles a beak, or a nose.

In environments where insectivorous primates are present, we find that silk moths with two eye-spots show a greater resemblance to these insectivores than they do to owls. The moths with eye-spots on their hind-wings tend to fall to the ground when disturbed; there the fore-wings blend with the fallen leaves and the hind-wings are displayed often with a central dark area outlined by a paler circle that resembles the eye of a nocturnal animal. An additional defence that these remarkable moths have is to mimic a stinging insect, bending the abdomen downwards so that the yellowish areas of the intersegmental membranes are exposed, suggesting the banded abdomen of a wasp or hornet. The abdomen is flexed to and fro in imitation of stinging movements.

In another type of silk moth wing pattern the fore-wings are more or less identical with the hind-wings so that four eyes of equal size are on display. This may be a way of presenting a supernormal stimulus, or of producing the painful illusion of double vision, shown on page 155, which I suggested protects the peacock butterfly from vertebrate predators. These aspects of perception do not trouble us for the reasons explained earlier: we have a highly complex system of image analysis that relies on a lot of remembered features, but image analysis in animals, you will recall from earlier chapters, starts with the simple abstracted sign stimuli that act like simple keys to unlock a fixed response.

Yet another group of silk moths has no large eye-spots; these are replaced by four semitransparent 'windows' that may be oval in shape or almost triangular, like the eyes of Spiderman. They have always mystified biologists. One clue I have to their possible function comes from photographs of an Atlas moth (the largest moth in the world), which on emergence and for some days afterwards had an oily droplet in the centre of each window. This then looks like a three-dimensional eye with light reflected from the surface. As evidence of these droplets is never seen on specimens in collections, it may be only a means of protecting the newly emerged insect, which is very vulnerable before its exoskeleton hardens; after a few flights the droplets are lost.

There are other more convincing reasons why the triangular windows on the wings have evolved. They are transparent areas of the wings that are not covered by the fine scales that give colour to the rest of the wing, and they have long been a mystery to entomologists. What we

opposite: **An Asian silk moth (*Caligula simla*) showing the changes that take place as the moth changes its appearance to that of an owl on being disturbed. The fore-wings with simulated markings of primary feathers bear strong resemblances to bird wings**

above left: **White-faced scops owl (*Scops leucotus*)**

above right: **The giant silk moth (*Automeris excreta*) with eye-spots that resemble the eyes of an owl or other nocturnal predator**

The Madagascan moon moth, (*Argema mittrei*) with eye-spots that have contracted 'pupils' suggestive of the eyes of lemurs in daylight

find is that those silk moths that have large eye-spots rarely have windows as well, so in some way the windows are an alternative deterrent. Three scientists at the University of Costa Rica[vi] examined the windows in the wings of *Rothschildia lebeau*, known familiarly as the '*cuatro ventanas*' (four windows), under the stereoscopic electron microscope. The windows were completely transparent to light striking the wing surface at right angles, but when light was shone at them at an angle they changed to being totally reflective, and became mirrors instead of windows. This is curious because the glass-winged butterflies of neotropical forests have a roughened wing surface that prevents reflection, like non-reflective glass in a picture frame, so they are almost invisible from every angle. The four-window moth, however, has the windows covered with fine tubular hairs, which do just the opposite: they reflect back light falling on them from the side, making the windows like beacons. The scientists speculate that this phenomenon enables the males and females to detect each other by reflected moonlight.

Doubtless the ancient Mexicans were much more aware of the mirrors, as they should be more aptly called, when most of the ambient light in those days came from the moon, and reflections from them readily brought to mind obsidian knives. Obsidian can be very reflective, and archaeologists have found obsidian mirrors. However, it is much more likely that the insects' mirrors are part of a defence mechanism rather than a mate-finding one: chemical communication by pheromones is extremely well developed in all the silk moths and is one of the most efficient mate-finding mechanisms known.

The objects most likely to reflect moonlight are the teeth, beak or claws of other animals, and I suggest the triangular windows represent these features, or the eyes of nocturnal animals such as owls or carnivores. Many animals have a third eyelid, called the nictitating membrane, which covers the eye when the animal is sleeping; so an owl's eye, for example, instead of appearing as a dark centre with an orange or yellow iris, appears as a white surface. Perhaps more intriguingly, the eyes of many nocturnal predators have a *tapetum lucidum*, which is a light-reflecting layer behind the retina. By reflecting back the light that passes through to the back of the eye, the tapetum ensures that as much as possible of the light entering the eye falls on some part of the retina. The tapetum is visible as 'eye-shine' when you see a dog, fox or cat in car headlights or in the light of a torch, and the eyes then appear like mirrors. Photographs of alligators taken at night by torchlight even at a distance show points of light in the dark. Could the 'windows' of the moths be simulations of the tapetum, reflecting moonlight from the eyes of nocturnal predators?

If this is so, there is an intriguing possibility that the windows create an optical illusion of movement. As you change your position relative to a moth the windows will reflect light and appear opaque, until you are looking directly at the windows and then you will see straight through them. Move a bit further and they reflect again, so the eye appears to be blinking at you. This is suggested in the photograph on page 184 of the Asian silk moth, *Antheraea frithi*, which has circular windows resembling eyes on each wing. The fore-wing spots are transparent,

A *Rothschildia lebeau* moth showing partial reflection of light from the windows on the wings

above left: **Eye-shine in a fox: light reflected from the tapetum**

above right: **The silk moth (*Antheraea frithi*) showing one window on the fore-wings that is transparent viewed from the camera angle, and the other three which reflect light except for a small central area that resembles a pupil**

so you see the leaf colour through them, but the hind-wing spots, which are seen at a slightly different angle, are mostly occluded and look like open eyes with small pupils. An insect like this can appear to have any combination of its four 'eyes' open or shut depending on the point of view of the observer and the background illuminance, and the combination will change as the point of view changes. Furthermore, such silk moths often make rocking movements when disturbed, or move the wings up and down, so making it more likely that the eyes will appear to open and close.

Having arrived at this hypothesis, I was delighted to find a video sequence on the Internet site YouTube of *Rothschildia lebeau* which confirmed my idea beautifully. The remarkable change in reflectivity can be seen in video sequences taken with the camera panning around the moths.[vii] In this moth the windows are elongated, so that they appear like flashing fangs of a jaguar, or spread claws (see opposite). The same features are seen in a number of other moths, including the giant Atlas moth of South-East Asia, in which there is an unmistakeable impression of claws protruding from a pair of feet, and even of the silhouette of a bat or bird with half-extended wings behind that.

The North American Robin moth, *Hyalophora cecropia*, and its relative, *H. euryalus*, have windows which come to sharp points resembling teeth or claws, but when viewed upside-down the image changes dramatically to reveal the devilish face of a rodent-like creature. Here, the windows are able to serve a double purpose in creating illusions.

The renowned tropical biologist Daniel Janzen has described how well camouflaged *Rothschildia* is in tropical forest during the daytime, when it hangs from branches like dead leaves with the spots and irregular black tracery resembling decaying leaves infested with fungal pathogens.

> "R. lebeau *hangs suspended from twigs and branches during daylight hours, 'fervently wishing' to be overlooked by birds and monkeys. Male and female* R. lebeau *are highly edible to at least five species of birds and six species of mammals at Santa Rosa, and were rejected by no vertebrate to which one was offered. It is normal for 20 to 50 per cent of the male moths attracted to virgin females to have bird beak marks on their wings. Predation by vertebrates is undoubtedly one of the major causes of the short lives of* R. lebeau *adults (1-10 days)."[viii]

Clearly, to resist predators at night, the moths cannot rely upon the cryptic features that are visible during the daytime. In contrast, large eye-spots that have been evolved by moths that do not possess wing windows are probably more effective in daylight than they are at night. Hence there appear to have been two alternative evolutionary lines, one leading to moths with eye-spots simulating predator eyes as seen in daylight, and another to moths with reflecting windows that simulate teeth, claws, or 'eye-shine' in moonlight.

The Aztecs and Mayans of Central America had a rich pantheon of gods and goddesses, with a dauntingly complex mythology attached to them. This mythology is recorded in the manuscript

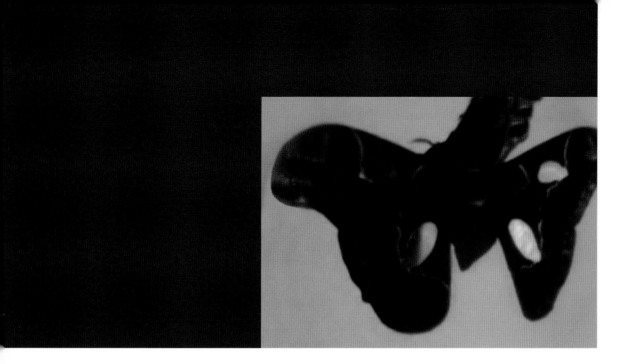

codices that survived the Spanish Conquest and, strikingly, includes a creation myth similar to that of Adam and Eve, also featuring a snake. Among the hundreds of deities is a goddess known as the Obsidian,[ix] or Obsidian Knife Moth goddess, Itzpapálotl.

Itzpapálotl is portrayed in several of the codices as a weird and fantastical figure that is, like many of the Aztec gods and goddesses, so foreign to our perception that she could be an alien creature from another planet. She is a chimaera – a grotesque imagining that surpasses anything produced by Hieronymus Bosch. Close inspection, however, reveals that she is a compendium of symbols that were highly meaningful to the Aztecs and the tribes that were there before them. Her head is formed by a skull symbol, representing death. Her limbs are those of a jaguar, with the claws of an eagle, her mantle is fringed with stones, obsidian sacrificial knives project from her body, and the wings extending from her arms bear four further obsidian knife images. Itzpapálotl is one of the so-called demons of darkness, an Aztec supernatural being believed to be one of the stars fallen from the sky. For the various tribes of the Valley of Mexico she was the mother goddess, a personification of the earth, goddess of war, hunting and sacrifice, and the protector of women who died in childbirth

Carlos Beutelspacher in his fascinating book *Las Mariposas entre los Antiguos Mexicanos* drew together all the information on butterflies and moths from the surviving codices, ceramics and stone carvings. Here, the obsidian 'butterfly' on which the goddess is based is said to be the giant silk moth known as *Rothschildia orizaba* and still known in Mexico as the *mariposa de navajas*, or knife butterfly. In Spanish, as in many languages of the world, butterflies and moths are not distinguished by separate names: they are both *mariposas*. Therefore, we should really say 'moth of the knives'. The insect acquired this name because of blade-shaped 'windows' found on each wing, which appear to flash in the light like the large obsidian knives used for carving open the chests of sacrificial victims and removing the still-beating heart. Obsidian is a form of glass, resulting from the melting of silica in the furious heat of Mexico's volcanoes. It can be shaped, like flint, to form sharp knives.

The presence of the knife images on the wings of a huge moth of the darkness evidently supported the web of beliefs that the souls of women who died in childbirth descended from the heavens taking away sacrificed hearts to sustain life and creation. Hence, to the moth icons of Itzpapálotl were added eagle claws to grasp the hearts, the skull head representing death, and in some figures, the head of the king vulture, the limbs of a jaguar, feather plumes of an eagle, of quetzal birds, symbols of fire, star symbols, a scorpion and an eagle owl, and a spider. Additional sacrificial knives protruded from various parts of the body. The face was sometimes portrayed with vertical stripes, symbolic of the demonic spirits or *Tzitzimime*, which were star deities that became demons and raided the earth in the night.

It is not surprising that the Spanish regarded Itzpapálotl and her numerous fellow deities as devils. The ancient Mexicans had created composite images that inspired the maximum fear

and dread. Representations of the most feared, poisonous and powerful animals were part of the mix – the jaguar, scorpion, eagle owl, spider, vulture, eagle, etc. The king vulture is so called because it is the largest of the vultures, flies higher than the rest, and when it lands to feed, other species of vulture give way to it. Yet it was deities such as Itzpapálotl that were the intermediaries that nourished the living lost souls returned from paradise, transfiguring them to form beautiful butterflies and hummingbirds to enjoy the flowers. It seems that, as in many of the world's religions, spreading belief in the existence of the devil or other terrifying supernatural creations was necessary to persuade the general populace to face the necessity of continual sacrifice and maintain the power of the priesthood.

The similarities between the nature and role of the patterns on the wings of the moth of the knives, and indeed many of the giant silk moths, and the images of the Aztec goddess are extraordinary. I believe that what the images of the goddess are designed to achieve, the colour patterns and designs on the wings of the giant silk moths moth also achieve by provoking confusion and fear in its potential predators.

First of all, Rothschildia moths have an eye-spot at the outer corner of each fore-wing. This was copied by the Aztecs onto portrayals of Itzpapálotl, possibly as a star sign. But in the moth, it is clearly an eye-spot. In the Atlas moth (Chapter 8) it is the eye of a snake, but try to make out a snakehead in the Rothschildias and that is not so easy. What the eye belongs to is the head of a caiman.[x] Going downwards from the wing tip a row of large teeth clearly marks out the snout of a caiman. The caiman image also appears in *Hyalophora* species (page 176), although there are various other possible interpretations of the design on the wing margin. In other words the design is natural surrealism and highly ambiguous – a puzzle for us, and conceivably for the moth's predators also.

Rothschildia jacobaeae showing the snout of a caiman on the wing borders

The Aztecs probably used the image of caiman more often in their mythology than has been realised. The famous plumed serpent god Quetzalcóatl shows a striking resemblance to the mythical beasts of European mythology and the dragons of the Orient. It is a fearsome-looking serpent with the plumes of the quetzal bird. The best-known stone carvings are those which adorn the Aztec Temple of Quetzalcóatl. But Quetzalcóatl has numerous large teeth – those of an alligator or crocodile, which a snake does not have, and a long broad snout. The venomous snakes typically have two large fangs at the front of the jaw and the rest of the jaw is occupied by small barb-like teeth projecting towards the throat, and a short snout, broad at the back to aid swallowing.

Quetzalcóatl is thus another composite figure, an alligator on a snake's body, with a crown of plume feathers from the precious and revered quetzal bird. We should bear in mind that the word serpent comes from the Latin *serpens*, which refers to all creeping and crawling animals. From the time of Aristotle, animals were classified by the way in which they moved rather than by affinities of anatomy and morphology as they are now, and 'serpent' would originally have applied not just to snakes, as it tends to now, but to reptiles in general.

It is likely that the Aztecs perceived the caiman image as such. It is visible in figures of Itzpapálotl in the Vatican Codex as an open jaw with large teeth and surmounted with stylised antennae. This would have led to an overlap in symbolic meaning between Quetzalcóatl and Itzpapálotl, the plumed serpent and the obsidian butterfly, which exists in accounts of these deities. For example, both represent the four quadrants of the compass: north, south, east and west, demanding sacrifices.

The Aztecs obviously extrapolated the triangular windows to include the red part of the wing marked by a black and white line, so this gave them the image of a knife blade

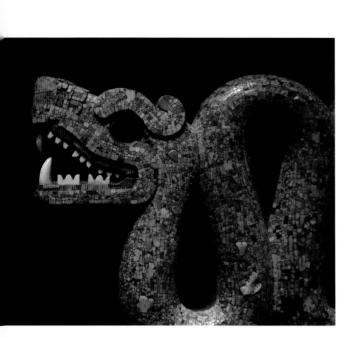

pointed at each end with one half coated in blood. The reddish colouring of the moth had another signification in addition to blood: that of fire, and the irregular flight of the insect gives the illusion of flickering flames. The Aztecs and the Chichimecs connected fire with the ascent of the soul to heaven, and the other butterfly goddess Xochiquétzal (a true butterfly), modelled on a tiger swallowtail (most likely, according to Beutelspacher,[xi] the three-tailed tiger swallowtail, *Papilio multicaudata*) was particularly associated with fire. The name, according to Beutelspacher, comes from *Xóchitl*, meaning 'flower' and *Quetzalli*, meaning 'beautiful'; but according to another interpretation the meaning is 'flower-bird beautiful butterfly', thus conflating the image of bird and butterfly. Her image was often painted with headdresses of plumes of the sacred quetzal bird.

As well as being the goddess of love, of flowers and a representation of beauty, Xochiquétzal was also the goddess of war. She was sometimes represented as a figure uniting opposites, bearing fire as a symbol of war, alongside a symbol of flowing water. Duran, writing in the nineteenth century, recorded the annual October ceremony of 'The farewell to the roses', when everybody and every place were garlanded with flowers, which were then sacrificed as a ritual of preparation for the hardships of the approaching winter. This was a festival in honour of Xochiquétzal who received all the flowers. Almost five hundred years later, one of our greatest poets drew on similar metaphors of fire and the rose writing about the Holy Spirit and Christ:

"*All manner of thing shall be well*
When the tongues of flames are in-folded
Into the crowned knot of fire
And the fire and the rose are one"
T.S. Eliot, *Little Gidding, Four Quartets*

above: **The Aztec goddess Itzpapálotl, from the Vatican Codex**

top left: **Head of Quetzalcóatl, the plumed serpent, part of a double-headed pectoral believed to have been presented to Hernán Cortés by Moctezuma. British Museum**

After the death of Moctezuma at the hands of the Conquistadors, his priests sacrificed butterflies in fires. The many thousands of human sacrifices over the centuries of their civilisation had failed to sustain their god-king and magnificent city. They had taken leave of their most valued symbols, the roses, the fire and the butterflies. The precious butterflies that symbolised for them beauty and spiritual life were used as messengers of last resort in the hope that all would then be well.

There is a legend of the ancient Maya, the origins of which are obscure, that the source of all energy and creation in the universe lies in an unknowable god, Hunab-ku, who has his domain in the Pleiades, in a star group now known as the 'butterfly' cluster – because the stars outline a butterfly. This was doubtless visible to the Mayans, who were expert astronomers: in fact it was described by Ptolemy, who had no telescope on which to rely. We now know that this cluster is right at the centre of our galaxy on the edge of what is possibly a black hole. The beauty of this legend is that the butterfly, which epitomises the beauty and elegance of nature, becomes also a symbol of the stars, of creation, and spiritual existence.

It is an astounding thought that the creatures that we see as among the most entrancing and graceful in the natural world, and which help us to understand our place in nature and the universe, were designed by evolutionary forces, not for our eyes, but to deceive their enemies. This brings us back to the place from which we started: why do we see in a rose, a macaw's feather or a swallowtail butterfly more than there is to see with the eye? Why does colour play so much on our emotions? Paul Gauguin, who was a supreme exponent of the use of colour, wrote,

> *"One does not use colour to draw but always to give the musical sensations which flow from itself, from its own nature, from its mysterious and enigmatic interior force."*[xii]

One attribute that sets man apart from animals is the appreciation of this mysterious force: we do not rely on colour and design to survive, as do animals, but as a doorway to pleasure and enlightenment. Why that should be remains an enduring mystery that takes us to the origin of man and the nature of creation.

opposite, top right: **A stone tablet from the Mexican Toltec culture, 850-1250 AD, uniting wings of a tiger swallowtail butterfly (associated with the goddess Xochiquétzal), eye-spots of a bull's eye moth (possibly representing the rain god Tlaloc), a Reptile's Eye hieroglyph (associated with Quetzelcóatl) and a water rail (symbol of the god Xochipilli, who was frequently accompanied by butterflies, flowers and birds)**

above left: **The three-tailed tiger swallowtail (*Papilio multicaudata*) which was used as the model for the Aztec goddess Xochiquétzal**

above right: **The three-tailed tiger swallowtail pictured on a Mixtec vase, 15th-16th century AD**

Index

Notes

Chapter 1

i   Bégouën, H."The Magic Origin of Palaeolithic Art". *Antiquity* 1929, 7
ii   Baring, A. & Cashford, J. *The Myth of the Goddess: Evolution of an Image.* Arkana/Penguin Books 1993
iii   Pliny, *Natural History*, Book 8, 33
iv   Leroi-Gourhan, A. *The Art of Prehistoric Man in Western Europe.* Thames & Hudson 1968
v   Gimbutas, M. *The Language of the Goddess*, Thames & Hudson 2001 and *Civilization of the Goddess*, HarperCollins 1991
vi   loc. cit
vii   Crane, Eva. *The Archaeology of Beekeeping*, Duckworth 1983
viii   Richards, O.W. – see discussion in Eva Crane, *Archaeology of Beekeeping*
ix   Loc.cit
x   Loc.cit
xi   Loc. cit
xii   Nougier, L.R. *La Preistoria.* Utet, Turin. 1982
xiii   Evans, quoted in Baring & Cashford
xiv   Tyler, P. *The Way of Ecstasy.* Canterbury Press 1997
xv   Manos-Jones, M. *The Spirit of Butterflies: Myth Magic and Art.* Abrams Inc. New York 2000

Chapter 2

i   Bates, H.W. *The Naturalist on the River Amazons.* John Murray 1873
ii   Wallace, A.R. *Travels on the Amazon and Rio Negro.* Warne 1853
iii   Graves, R. *The Greek Myths.* Folio Society 1996
iv   Figuier, L. *Les Insectes.* Librairie Hachette, Paris 1875
v   Wood, J.G. *The Illustrated Natural History III.* Routledge 1863
vi   In Dali, S. *The Secret Life of Salvador Dali.* Munich 1979
vii   Internet source
viii   Hill, S. *I'm the King of the Castle.* Penguin Books 1989

Chapter 3

i   See Royal Navy Internet site for this and related information
ii   Gimbutas, M. *The Language of the Goddess.* Thames & Hudson 2001
iii   *Holy Bible*, St.John 19:17
iv   Gledhill, Ruth. *The Times.* London 19 January 2005

Chapter 4

i   In Gombrich, E.H. *Art and Illusion.* Phaidon 1959
ii   N.Tinbergen's work is summarised in *The Animal and its World.* Allen & Unwin 1972; and *Curious Naturalists.* Country Life 1966
iii   The neurophysiology of vision is dealt with by various authors in *The Artful Eye*, ed. R. Gregory et al. Oxford University Press 1993
iv   In Barrow, J. *The Artful Universe.* Penguin 1997
v   Hubbard, J. "Middle Palaeolithic Art, Symbols, Mind". OriginsNet. Internet site
vi   Pliny, *Natural History* 29, xix.
vii   Loc. cit.
viii   See Walsh and Kulikowski in *The Artful Eye* (loc. cit.)
ix   Murdoch, I. *Metaphysics as a Guide to Morals.* Penguin 1992

Chapter 5

i   Torry & Miller, *The Capture of the Snark.* Richmond Review Library. (Internet)
ii   California Dept. of Agriculture Report. Internet source
iii   Hartcup, G. *Camouflage: A History of Concealment and Deception in War.* David & Charles 1979
iv   In Preston-Mafham, R. & K. *Butterflies of the World.* Blandford Press, London 1988
v   Thompson, D.W. *On Growth and Form.* Cambridge University Press 1992
vi   Miriam Rothschild had already spotted the resemblance of the head to a queen bee. See Rothschild, M. "Aide Memoire mimicry". *Ecological Entomology* 9, 1984, 311-319

Chapter 6

i   Grandin, T. & Johnson, C. *Animals in Translation.* Bloomsbury, London 2005
ii   Williams, D. *Nobody Nowhere.* Time Books, New York 1992
iii   Williams, D. *Autism and Sensing.* Jessica Kingsley 1998
iv   This is also the name given to the adult (winged) insect, sometimes also referred to as the 'perfect insect'
v   Simons, D.J & Chabris C.F. "Gorillas in our midst: sustained inattentional blindness for dynamic events". *Perception* 28, 1999, 1059-74
vi   LeDoux, J.E. *The Emotional Brain: The Mysterious Underpinnings of Emotional Life.* Simon & Schuster, New York 1998
vii   See Tilley, C. *Metaphor and Material Culture.* Blackwell 1999.
viii   Turner, T. "We are parrots", "Twins are birds." In J. Fernandez (ed), *Beyond Metaphor.* Stanford 1991 (quoted in Tilley, see above)
ix   J. Harrod's publications are available on the Internet from www.origins.net
x   Leslie Williamson, personal communication

Chapter 7

i   Howse, P.E. & Allen, J.A. "Satyric mimicry: the evolution of apparent imperfection". *Proceedings of the Royal Society*, 257 1994
ii   Dittrich, W. et al. "Imperfect Mimicry. A Pigeon's Perspective". *Proceedings of the Royal Society*, 251 1993
iii   Victoria & Albert Museum website
iv   Gombrich, E.H. in *Illusion in Nature and Art* (Ed. Gregory, R.L. & Gombrich, E.H.) Duckworth 1973
v   "Darwin nearly failed to evolve in print". Shirley English in *The Times*, 27th April 2007
vi   Gombrich, E.H. *Art and Illusion.* Phaidon 1959
vii   Krusche, "Ambiguity in Perception". Indiana State University internet publication
viii   Venkatesha, M.G. et al. "Protective devices of the carnivorous butterfly, *Spalgis epius*". *Current Science*, 87, 5 2004
ix   Rahav, G. & Weiss, A.T. *Chest.* June 1990
x   Costa-Neto, E. M. & Pacheco, J. M. "'Head of snake, wings of butterfly, and body of cicada': impressions on the lantern fly (Hemiptera: Fulgoridae) in the village of Pedra Branca, Bahia State, Brazil". *Journal of Ethnobiology*, 23 (1): 23-46 2003

Chapter 8

i   Morris, R. & D. *Men and Snakes.* Hutchinson 1965
ii   Agras et al. "The epidemiology of common fears and phobias". *Comprehensive Psychiatry*, 10, 151 1969
iii   loc. cit.
iv   *Holy Bible*, Exodus 7:8-12
v   Hughes, B. *Helen of Troy: Goddess, Princess and Whore.* Vintage 2006
vi   Sagan, C. *The Dragons of Eden: Speculations on the Evolution of Human Intelligence.* Hodder & Stoughton, London 1977
vii   Seyfarth, R.M., Cheney, D.L. & Marler, P. "Vervet monkey alarm calls: Semantic communication in a free-ranging primate". *Animal Behaviour* 28:1070-1094 1980
viii   Crockford, C. & Boesch, C. "Context-specific calls in wild chimpanzees, *Pan troglodytes* versus analysis of barks". *Animal Behaviour*, 66, 115-126 2003. Cheney, D. & Seyforth, R. "Constraints and preadaptations in the earliest stages of language evolution". *The Linguistic Review*, 22, 135-15 2005
ix   *The Observer*, 1 October 2006
x   Oehman, A. & Mineka, S. "The malicious serpent: Snakes as a prototypical stimulus for an evolved module of fear". *Current directions in Psychological Science*, 12 (1) 5-9 2000
xi   Matthews, J. & C. *The Element Encyclopaedia of Mythical Creatures.* Harper 2005

Chapter 9

i   The staring eyes and large teeth are also a feature of Hindu and Indonesian totemic masks
ii   Edgar, Robin. "Eye in the Sky". Internet publication
iii   An explanation for the extra markings is given by Robert Temple in *The Crystal Sun* (Century, London 2000). He claims that the eye is compounded of Egyptian hieroglyphic signs for

mathematical fractions which reveal the value of the Comma of Pythagoras, a number that enters into many calendrical, architectural and other physical measurements
iv   Ed. Gregory, R.L. & Gombrich, E.H. *Illusion in Nature and Art.* Duckworth 1973
v   Porphyrios, D. *Classical Architecture.* Papadakis 2006
vi   Paine, S. *Amulets: A World of Secret Powers, Charms and Magic.* Thames & Hudson 2004
vii   Carrington, D. *Dream-Hunters of Corsica.* Weidenfeld & Nicolson 1995
viii   I was told in Sardinia, while writing this book, of a man who had a serious skin rash, known locally as 'St.Anthony's fire'. His doctor referred him to a woman in the nearby village who dealt with the Evil Eye. She cured him, and antibiotics were not needed
ix   Morris, D. *Watching: Encounters with Humans and Other Animals.* Max Press, London 2006
x   Menzies, Gavin. 1421 *The Year that China discovered the World.* Bantam 2003
xi   Sirén, O. *Chinese painting: Leading Masters and Principles.* New York, 1956-8. Quoted in Michaelson C. *Gilded Dragons.* British Museum Press 1999
xii   Eibl-Eibesfeldt, I. & Strachan. G. *Love and Hate: The Natural History of Basic Behaviour Patterns.* Holt Rinehart & Winston 1972
xiii   Sample, I. "The eyes have it for making people behave more honestly". *The Guardian*, 28 February 2007
xiv   Blest, A.D. "The function of eyespot patterns in the Lepidoptera". *Behaviour* 11, 209 1957
xv   Report in *The Observer* newspaper 1992
xvi   Robertson, K.A. & Monteiro, A. "Female *Bicyclus anynana* butterflies choose males on the basis of their dorsal UV-reflective eyespot pupils". *Proceedings of the Royal Society* B 272, 1541–1546 2005

Chapter 10

i   For an excellent discussion on bird vision see the university internet site: http://people.eku.edu/RICHTISONG/avian_biology.html
ii   Bennett, A.T.D. "A Bird's-eye View". *Nature*, 445, 150 2007
iii   Church, S et al."Ultraviolet cues affect the foraging behaviour of blue tits". *Proceedings of the Royal Society*, B 265 1509 1998
iv   Eliot, T.S. *The Four Quartets.* T.S.Eliot: Collected Poems. Faber & Faber 1963
v   Bates, H.W. *The Naturalist on the River Amazons.* John Murray 1863
vi   Quoted by Alfred Werner in *Butterflies and Moths.* Deutsch, London 1956
vii   Vukusic, P., Sambles J.R., Lawrence C.R. & Wooton R.J. "Quantified interference and diffraction in single *Morpho* butterfly scales". *Proceedings of the Royal Society* B. 1999, 266, 1403
viii   In Crotch, W.J.B. *A Silk Moth Rearer's Handbook.* Amateur Entomologists' Society, London 1956
ix   Seckel, A. *Incredible Visual Illusions.* Arcturus, London 2004

Chapter 11

i   Baring, A. & Cashford, J. *The Myth of the Goddess: Evolution of an Image.* Penguin Books 1993
ii   In Beutelspacher, C. *Las Mariposas entre los Antiguos Mexicanos.* UNAM Mexico 1996
iii   Gimbutas, M.
iv   Loc. Cit.
v   Hinde, R.A. *Animal Behaviour.* McGraw-Hill 1966
vi   Hernández-Chavarría, F., Hernández, A. & Sittenfeld, A. "The 'windows', scales and bristles of the tropical moth *Rothschildia lebeau* (Lepidoptera: Saturniidae)". *Revista de Biologia Tropical*, Costa Rica 2007
vii   There is one such sequence posted on the Internet on YouTube by "rayywang" 2007: http://www.youtube.com/watch?v=4w7Bju3u_Vw
viii   Janssen, D. *Bull. Am Ent. Soc.*
ix   Beutelspacher, C. op. cit
x   'Caiman' is the name given to neotropical alligators
xi   Loc. cit.
xii   From Gauguin's manuscript "Diverses Choses, 1896-7". Tahiti. Quoted in Chipp, H.B. *Theories of Modern Art.* Univ. of California Press 1986